JUSTICE and the INTIFADA

JUSTICE and the INTIFADA

Palestinians and Israelis Speak Out

Edited by
Kathy Bergen, David Neuhaus,
and Ghassan Rubeiz

Friendship Press • New York
WCC Publications • Geneva

Published by Friendship Press
Editorial Offices: 475 Riverside Drive, New York, NY 10115
Distribution Offices: P.O. Box 37844, Cincinnati, OH 45222-0844

and

WCC Publications
150 route de Ferney, 1211 Geneva 20, Switzerland

Manufactured in the United States of America

Library of Congress Cataloging-in-Publication Data

Bergen, Kathy.
Justice and the Intifada : Palestinians and Israelis speak out / interviews by Kathy Bergen, David Neuhaus, and Ghassan Rubeiz.
p. cm.
Includes bibliographical references.
ISBN 0-377-00237-2
1. Intifada, 1987- —Public opinion. 2. Jewish-Arab relations—1973- —Public opinion. 3. Palestinian Arabs—Interviews. 4. Israelis–Interviews. 5. Public opinion—Israel. 6. Public opinion—West Bank. 7. Public opinion–Gaza Strip. I. Neuhaus, David. II. Rubeiz, Ghassan. III. Title.
DS119.75.B47 1991
956.04–dc20 91-20506
CIP

WCC Publications ISBN 2 8254 10584

Contents

Part 3: WOMEN

Part 4: RELIGIOUS PERSPECTIVES

Dateline

1882	Beginning of modern Jewish immigration to Palestine
1897	First Zionist Congress, in Basel
1917	Issuing of the Balfour Declaration
1918	The whole of Palestine occupied by the Allied forces
1936	Outbreak of the Arab revolt against British rule and Zionism
1939–45	Second World War and extermination of six million Jews in Europe
1947	Palestine problem submitted to the United Nations
	November 29: Decision to partition Palestine between Jews and Palestinian Arabs
	Outbreak of hostilities in Palestine
1948	April 9: Massacre at Deir Yassin
	May 15: Declaration of the State of Israel
	Outbreak of 1948 war
1950	West Bank united with Jordan; Gaza Strip administered by Egypt
1956	Outbreak of 1956 war; Kfar Qasim massacre
1964	Founding of the Palestine Liberation Organization (PLO)
1967	Outbreak of the 1967 war; Israeli military occupation of West Bank, Gaza Strip, and Golan Heights
1973	Outbreak of 1973 war

1978	Signing of Camp David Accords by U.S. President Carter, Egyptian President Sadat, and Israeli Prime Minister Begin
1982	Israeli invasion of Lebanon
	Sabra and Shatila massacre
1987	December 9: Outbreak of the intifada
1988	November 14: Declaration of the independent State of Palestine
1989	April 2: Yasser Arafat elected president of Palestine

Acknowledgments

This book is inspired by the years of contact the editors have had with Israelis and Palestinians — in particular, those who have struggled for the realization of their rights, those who have struggled for peace, and those who have sacrificed for the sake of justice. We gratefully acknowledge the role of Janet Gunn in the initial stages of the book, in formulating the focuses, and in participating in some of the early interviews. We also thank Wafiq Abu Sido for serving as our contact with the Gaza Strip. We express our appreciation of the assistance offered us by Yahya Hijazi, Elaine Lindouwer, Zoghbi Zoghbi, and Lydia Maria Goymer. Finally, we are most grateful to all those who were interviewed; they were generous with their time and free with their thoughts.

Introduction

The intifada, the recent Palestinian uprising, broke out in December 1987 as a spontaneous and general declaration of Palestinians in the areas under Israeli military rule that they would no longer live under Occupation. Over three years have passed since then, and we must ask ourselves, Can we hear what is being said? Can we hear the Palestinians who are saying no to the Israeli Occupation? Can we hear the Israelis who are in anguish over their future? Both sides demand justice; both desperately need peace.

Many books have been written about the Palestinian-Israeli conflict. As this book began to take shape, we knew that we wanted to focus on the intifada and to allow voices to speak which in some cases, had not been readily heard in the West. For the more than four decades of this nagging conflict, the West has been concerned with formulating a peace settlement. The word "justice" has often been uttered in the same breath as the word "peace." "Peace and justice" — the ease with which these terms have been regularly combined has, in fact, turned the phrase into a cliché, which blurs the necessity of each one and suggests that justice follows as an almost automatic consequence of peace. The intifada has given new edges to this smooth phrase. The realization that *there is no lasting peace without justice* has replaced reliance on the old cliché.

Every Palestinian has been affected by the intifada in some way. Many families have lost loved ones or have had members imprisoned, detained, or interrogated. Homes have been destroyed, orchards uprooted, land confiscated. Those who have escaped direct loss have been affected by the closure of schools and universities and the disruption of news agencies and national institutions. All Palestinians have been affected by the curfews that have frequently been imposed on whole towns and villages and on whole areas of Palestine/the Occupied Territories. The Palestinian national leadership as well as the leadership of the Islamic movement have initiated general strikes that have brought life to a standstill.

Every Israeli has been affected by the intifada in some way. Regular and reserve soldiers have been called up for long periods of military service in Palestine/the Occupied Territories in order to crush the intifada. These men have suffered the assault of an enraged civilian population as well as the psychological trauma of being occupiers. The Israeli peace camp, horrified by the brutality of the Israeli army, took to the streets, and vigils, demonstrations, and petitions against the Occupation became a regular feature of Israeli life. The Israeli economy has been crippled by the expense of maintaining high military presence in these areas. Resources essential for maintaining a reasonable standard of living, sufficient health care, minimal education, and essential social services have been channelled into the maintenance of the Occupation. Israeli society has been polarized, leading to the collapse of the government and political paralysis, and many Israelis across the political spectrum have become despairing and disillusioned.

Concerning the Middle East, extreme political opinions have more access to the media than do sober voices. Extremism is often dramatic, vicarious, cathartic, and appealing in a region where emotions are loud and tribalism in politics is common. Political leaders exploit the public by nourishing their personal images, offering the crowds maximalist language, categorical judgments, stereotypes, and easy solutions to complex problems.

The intifada is a major phenomenon that is being monitored daily by the mass media. It is being compared with other points of struggle in Africa, Latin America, and Eastern Europe. There has been increasing interest in the Israel-Palestine conflict but little international response to the concrete demands of the Palestinian people. Third World solidarity with Palestinians who are denied their political and human rights is undermined by superpower patronage and relations of economic dependency. The countries of Europe have been increasingly vocal in responding to Palestinian protest but have displayed customary caution in evolving a material response to the concrete demands.

The USSR has been virtually overshadowed in the diplomatic decision making concerning the Israel-Palestine conflict. It has moreover complicated the conflict by suddenly giving freedom to its Jewish citizens to emigrate without helping in the creation of alternatives for their residence in places other than Israel. Instead of being provided with passports, Jews have been transferred to Israel with no option of return to their country of origin or of going to some Western country. The immigration of Soviet Jews to Israel indicates that any future settlement of the Israel-Palestine conflict will need to include the question of the right of return of both Jews and Palestinians.

Government and public opinion in the United States play a critical role in the conflict. Despite the shift in attitude among many Americans toward the Palestinians under Occupation, this support falls short of political pressure on Israel. The U.S. State Department has not been able to influence Israel to allow Palestinians to choose their own representatives for the peace negotiations proposed by the Shamir plan. The State Department is "enabling" both sides, but not with equal means. To the Israelis the United States offers billions of dollars a year in unconditional aid. To the Palestinians it offers low-key diplomatic contact so that they feel that they are not totally excluded from the negotiation process. Unless Washington changes its strategy in facilitating the peace process, the suffering will continue and the tension will rise with unpredictable consequences.

Before the intifada, the Occupation had been a status quo. Palestinians had struggled to survive in spite of the numerous obstacles placed in their path. Israelis had assumed that their lives could continue as before, despite the state of perpetual war with the Palestinians. The two peoples had become economically intertwined. The intifada, however, has challenged what had become the status quo for both.

Kathy Bergen is a Canadian who has lived among Palestinians in the Occupied Territories, one familiar with their way of life and listening closely to their voices and their needs. David Neuhaus is an Israeli of South African and German background, a political science student at the Hebrew University in Jerusalem, proficient in both Hebrew and Arabic. Ghassan Rubeiz is a Lebanese social scientist, secretary of the Middle East desk at the World Council of Churches, Geneva. The editors have witnessed the intifada from the beginning and have seen how it has affected both societies. They have rejoiced in the potential for change that is inherent in the new situation and have grieved over the shocking price in human lives and human souls. In collaborating on this book, the editors drew on personal friendship as well as the sensitivities that have evolved in their involvement with the two societies in conflict.

In selecting the interviewees, we attempted to preserve certain delicate balances within the two societies, Israeli and Palestinian. We interviewed figures from both societies who have become well known as spokespersons for various perspectives as well as those who are unknown, the unheard voices. Many of the interviews were conducted in Arabic or Hebrew, as we attempted to get beyond the superficiality that often results from people trying to express themselves in a foreign language. The intifada has seen a surge of women's activity — women both as spokespersons for mixed-gender groups and as participants in groups specifically for women — and therefore hearing women speak for themselves became a priority.

Within Palestinian society the balances we attempted to reflect were on numerous levels. First, we tried to find interviewees who voice the plurality of political and ideological perspectives within the Palestinian national movement. Second, the interviews are geographically distributed over all areas of Palestine/Israel — interviews from the West Bank, from the Gaza Strip, and from Palestinian citizens of Israel. Third, we have tried to reflect the proportionate religious-communal heterogeneity of Palestinian society, an Islamic majority with various Christian and Druze religious minorities.

Within Israeli society we also tried to give expression to various perspectives. Although we have stressed, in our choice of interviewees, individuals and collectives who are peacemakers, embarked upon a search for a just solution to the conflict, we believed it essential to hear the voice of the Israeli right wing too. In choosing spokespersons for various issues, we have tried to illuminate also the relations between Ashkenazi and Oriental Jews, between secular and religious Jews, and between Jewish and Palestinian Arab citizens of Israel.

In organizing the interviews, we present first the views of the most immediate parties to the conflict. Those at the forefront of the struggle are, on the one hand, the young Palestinian men and women in the refugee camps, towns, and villages in Palestine/the Occupied Territories, and, on the other hand, the Israeli soldiers patrolling these areas as well as the Israelis who have settled there. Thrust into the forefront of this conflict are the new immigrants to Israel, and foremost among these are the Jews from the Soviet Union who have been arriving throughout the period of the intifada. Then we present interviews with Israelis and Palestinians who, in spite of the hardships they are facing, are resisting the Occupation and are calling for a political solution to the conflict through dialogue and compromise that will lead to a lasting peace. Next we hear from women who struggle for justice and are unable to separate the struggle against the Occupation from the struggle for equality for women. Finally, we listen to Israeli Jews and Palestinian Muslims and Christians, clergy and laity, who throw light both on the religious perspectives involved in the struggle for the Holy Land and on their respective religious traditions of justice.

We travelled the length and breadth of Israel/Palestine collecting these interviews. We visited Palestinian refugee camps and Israeli settlements and spoke with the young and the old, men and women, religious and secular, the doctrinaire and the open. Everywhere we went, we were offered the generous hospitality of those who had agreed to share their time with us. The collection is not comprehensive or all-inclusive, yet by listening carefully to the individual voices, we may gain a fuller understanding of the complex tensions of this chapter of a prolonged and mournful conflict.

Postscript

A year has passed since we completed the interviews in this collection. It has been a year of destruction, devastation, and agony for the entire Middle East. In August 1990 the Iraqi army invaded Kuwait, annexing the oil-rich principality, claiming it as part of the historical Iraqi homeland. Five months later a U.S.-led coalition, including many European countries and a number of Arab countries too, began a full frontal attack on Iraq to liberate Kuwait from Iraqi control.

The conflict between Iraq and the U.S.-dominated alliance had a strong impact upon the Israeli-Palestinian conflict. Once again it revealed the distance between the two sides. While Israel identified itself with the coalition against Iraq, Palestinians opposed the U.S.-initiated intervention in the internal affairs of the Arab world. This distance became an almost unbridgeable chasm when Israel became a target of Iraqi missile attacks during the hostilities. Israelis were outraged by these attacks, as they saw themselves as peripheral observers in the war. Palestinians, and many other Arabs, saw Israel as fully involved in this war and a main cause of the instability in the region. While Israelis celebrated coalition victories, Palestinians, placed under military curfew for the duration of the war, mourned the massive destruction wrought by the coalition on the Arab heartland. Processes of dialogue between Israelis active in the peace movements and Palestinians ground to a halt. Israelis were outraged by Palestinian support for Iraq and President Saddam Hussein; Palestinians were outraged by American and Israeli determination to liberate Kuwait while nothing had been done to liberate the Occupied Territories after thirteen years of Occupation and three years of intifada.

Israelis perceived Saddam Hussein as a greedy and bloodthirsty tyrant. The campaign to demonize Saddam was no doubt based upon his record as a totalitarian dictator but obscured the fact that Saddam's military prowess was the consequence of shortsighted superpower policy in the Middle East. Seeking a bulwark against the Shiite Islamic resurgence embodied in Iran, Iraq had been supplied with weapons of mass destruction. American policy, relying on the divisive cleavages within the Arab world, had created a coalition supported by numerous Arab countries, including Saudi Arabia, Egypt, and Syria, who found themselves indirectly linked with Israel in the attempts to destroy Saddam and liberate Kuwait.

Palestinians and many millions throughout the Arab world perceived Saddam in a different light. Saddam linked his irredentist claims on Kuwait with promises to execute a more equitable distribution of assimilated Arab wealth. When faced with the stubborn American position to his occupation of Kuwait, Saddam linked his own future withdrawal to an inclusive settlement of all Middle Eastern territorial disputes, including the Israeli occupation of Palestine. These statements were understandably welcomed by Palestinians and the PLO but they were also welcomed by millions throughout the Arab world who popularly saw Saddam as a leader promising a better future, willing to say no to the West even in the face of a massive military threat. Palestinians welcomed the Iraqi insistence on linkage that made the Palestinian question a central issue in the Gulf crisis.

The war has ended and Kuwait has been liberated. International legitimacy has been restored and the UN resolutions that were legislated have been implemented fully. While Iraq is still suffering the consequences of the disastrous war, Kuwait is being rebuilt with Western aid. Yet the Occupied Territories have not been liberated. International legitimacy has not been restored and the UN resolutions that have been legislated over the past twenty-three years have not even been partially implemented. On the contrary Israeli settlement of the Occupied Territories continues, while Israeli restrictions on Palestinian life there have increased. Palestinians and many Israelis too are dumbfounded that U.S. determination to liberate countries occupied by military force should be restricted to oil rich Kuwait alone.

And so, although these interviews dealt with the reality of the Israeli-Palestinian conflict before the Gulf War, the most startling aspect of this reality after the Gulf War is that the basic issues remain exactly as they were. Israeli attempts to transform the demographic, agricultural, educational, political, and social realities of the Occupied Territories increase. Palestinian attempts to resist these attempts through the intifada continue. The two sides are locked in battle and the attempts by the American administration to influence the political process, leading eventually to dialogue, have had no effect thus far. The new perspective on this agonizing struggle is the clarity of the double standard with which the West has judged this conflict. The urgency with which the West sought to liberate Kuwait necessitates at least equivalent resolution and determination to resolve the Israeli-Palestinian conflict.

PART 1

THOSE AT THE FRONT

Ali, Hassan, Umar, and Uthman

Young men and women — the shabab — in the Palestinian refugee camps, villages, and towns in the Occupied Territories constitute the activist core of the intifada leadership. They know nothing but life under Occupation, yet the intifada is, to a large extent, about their hopes, dreams, and aspirations. Since December 1987 they have been risking their lives daily, defying the Israeli soldiers. Hundreds have been shot dead or beaten to death; thousands have been wounded and tens of thousands have been imprisoned.

In a Palestinian refugee camp on the West Bank, we spoke with four young men — Ali (twenty-three years old), Hassan (twenty), Umar (eighteen), and Uthman (twenty-one).

Editors: We are interested in what you have to say about the issue of justice.

Ali: Before the intifada began, we, the Palestinian people, were already convinced of the justice of our struggle, and it made no difference whether the world was with us or against us. For the rest of the world, other problems were more pressing. Because of the intifada, however, the entire world has now been able to see what is happening in this land. Possibly now some nations see the nature of the Occupation here and see the Palestinian people demanding their rights, demanding a state and possessing a historical right to this land. Possibly they see that another people came as conquerors to this land, saying, "A land without a people for a people without a land" — and then under this slogan these conquerors expelled the people from their land.

Many nations were formerly against the Palestinian people, saying that we were a nation of terrorists and our organization a terrorist organization. The intifada, though — in which all classes of Palestinians have participated — has brought to light the nature of the Occupation. Finally the world has understood that there is a problem of justice. Here are people who have a right to a state, to independence, to choose their own form of rule, and to liberate their land. This became the number-one problem in the world.

Hassan: As a result of the Second World War and what Hitler did, the whole world — especially the countries of Western Europe and most of the people in America — sympathized with the State of Israel. Zionist propaganda has presented the Israeli people as those who have suffered injustice because another people want to throw them into the sea. But the intifada has announced to the entire world that the Palestinian people are a peaceful people, demanding their rights of a state on their own land, not the land of someone else.

I did not come here from the Soviet Union or from Germany. I am a member of this people; I was born here, and my roots go back thousands of years. I did not come here from the Soviet Union a few days ago saying this is my state. The intifada has announced to one and all that the Palestinian people have suffered injustice and are now demanding a simple right: to be allowed to have their state like all the nations of the world — with dignity, free of the injustice of an occupation or the exploitation of another state.

Umar: The intifada has helped a great deal to publicize the Palestinian problem in the international arena and to increase the consciousness of the world. It has clearly shown who has suffered — contrary to Zionist propaganda, which has presented us as united against the Jews, just waiting to kill them and throw them into the sea. The intifada has clarified exactly who is being wiped out, who is being killed. It has publicized our just demands and our right to live in our independent state, on our land, on our national soil. We have a historic right concerning this. No Jew who came a few days ago from Argentina, the Soviet Union, or Europe and who becomes a soldier has the right to come and expel me from my land.

Ali: Since we were born here, as were our parents and our grandparents, do we not have the right to establish our state here? We did not emigrate from another country and settle here. We are here, as were the grandparents of our grandparents. It is our right to have a state on our land.

Eds.: Many Israelis say that once a Palestinian state is established in the territories occupied by Israel in 1967, the injustice against the Palestinian people will be corrected. Do you agree?

Ali: It's hard to answer this question. Most of the left-wing Israelis in the peace movement are Zionists and believe that Zionism is a national liberation movement for the Jewish people. They believe that they too have a right to a state and the right to live in it. Their central concern is security for that state. For this very reason they agree to a Palestinian state.

Not a single left-wing movement, however, formulates its vision of such a state in the West Bank and the Gaza Strip as a state in the full sense of the word, one with its own army and full independence. Throughout history human beings have demanded freedom, which would be absent from such a nonstate, just as it would be absent from Jordan if people did not feel free there. The feeling of freedom is the important thing, not the state. What is the value of such a state, if it has the name State of Palestine but is just a name? We would accept only a completely independent state. Yet if the Zionists agree to this, they would be retreating from everything they believe in. There is no way the Zionist movement can accept this type of state with its present program.

Uthman: The goal of the intifada was very clear right from the beginning: freedom and independence, dignity for humanity. This dignity disappeared as a result of the Occupation. But now, with the intifada, the people are feeling a little happier. They feel that now they are fighting. They have understood that we cannot stop. Now they will be satisfied with nothing less than a completely independent Palestine with an army and all the trappings of a state.

Eds.: You, here in this refugee camp in the West Bank, are part of a problem that goes back to 1948.

Ali: We recognize the Right of Return: the refugees' right to return to the land that was taken from them. I personally am willing to return to my village and live as a part of a national Arab minority under Israeli rule. This is my right. The Jews have their own Law of Return. According to Zionist logic, any Jew in the Soviet Union has the right to "return" to the Land of Israel and could live anywhere in this land, even on the West Bank. But it is my right as a Palestinian refugee who was expelled forty years ago to return to my village.

Even if we did have the power to take all the land, we need to think of the human problem. Some of the Jews who have been here for many years have cut contact with the countries from which they came. There is no possibility to send a Polish Jew back to Poland, for example. We, as Palestinians, who believe in the justice of our cause, could we now expel people once again? They were the victims of Hitler, and now we are their victims. We became the victims' victims. I refuse to accept this pattern.

Hassan: I have a right to a state in the territories conquered in 1967, not what Shamir or other members of the Zionist movement might have in mind for me. But I cannot forget Jaffa and Haifa, or my village Z., where I desire to go. Yet I have to take into account the Jews who are living there now. What am I supposed to do with them? I cannot send them back to the Soviet Union. In the Palestinian covenant the Jews who lived in Palestine before 1917, before the European Jewish immigrations to Palestine, are recognized as part of Palestine. We lived with these Jews, and we thought of them as Palestinians. Possibly they had a different religion, maybe even a different language, but they were considered Palestinians. Jews who are born here have the right to live here, just as I do, and the right to participate in the life of the state, just like any other person. So what are we supposed to do with these people who are here now — and there are millions of them? Can we really throw them into the sea? I have no wish to kill them; they are people like everyone else.

We will always remember what the Jews did to us, but just because they have killed Palestinian children, that does not mean that one day I will kill Jewish children. My attitude is that all who want to live with me are most welcome, even a thousand years from now. They can come and live in my state, an independent Palestinian state. They can live with me with full dignity and respect like any other person; there will be no difference between Palestinian and Jew.

Eds.: What about the collaborators?

Umar: The collaborators have lost their humanity, their ability to love. Can they reform themselves? They should just be killed.

Hassan: The Israelis are showing films about the killing of collaborators to demonstrate that the Palestinians are terrorists. Maybe people are influenced by these pictures. Yet in other films they might see soldiers of a certain army killing collaborators who have betrayed their people, and that they would accept.

Uthman: A saying goes, If I see a collaborator and a soldier, who will I kill? — the collaborator. As in any country under occupation, there are many collaborators. These agents commit many dirty acts; they ruin many people, many girls; they kill people involved in the struggle and serve as interrogators in the prisons. Killing such collaborators is an act of justice. We have seen it most in Nablus and the Gaza Strip, and then afterward it spread to Qalqiliya and Jenin and also to the south.

Many collaborators are simply stupid; they do it to get a permit, a passport, or a little money. Often they express a willingness to repent. Generally, though, it is very difficult for collaborators to repent and cut their contacts with the secret police. If they do, the secret police will make problems for them. Within the secret police there is a special section for the collaborators. If they ever tried to cut contact, they would find it very difficult and would return to the police.

Before it kills a collaborator, the national movement is usually very cautious and also cautions the collaborator. If a collaborator carries weapons and shoots at people during demonstrations in the presence of the army, the national movement puts this collaborator on trial in what is called the revolutionary court. The decision of the court is then carried out.

It is of no use to try certain collaborators who are responsible for murdering others. The strike forces give the command that anyone who sees them has the authority to kill them. When people like these are killed, the people pass out sweets and sing. The important thing is that the people accept the killings. When someone is imprisoned, the first thing the mothers do is climb up on the wall and shout out: "God take revenge on all the collaborators! Why, O God, don't you send people to kill them and destroy their homes?" Not just the mothers speak like this, everyone does.

Eds.: How do you think the intifada has created a revolution in the status of men and women in Palestinian society?

Ali: Some areas in Palestine preserve tradition, and others do so to a lesser extent. In areas dominated by right-wing groups, such as Hebron, which is known as a very conservative and religious area, the participation of the women in the Palestinian struggle is minor. The men there do not help the women to participate actively in the Palestinian struggle and are not interested in realizing woman's rights.

In other areas, the intifada has done a lot for women. In Bethlehem or Ramallah, for example, women have had a big role in the Palestinian struggle. Political forces active in Bethlehem are more pluralist than in a conservative place like Hebron and therefore give the woman a greater role. In many areas of Bethlehem the left-wing forces clearly formulate equality for men and women as part of their ideology. The man there helps the woman in her role as a participant in the struggle instead of putting obstacles in her way. What has happened is that women have followed each other's example, and so the participation of women has grown.

Uthman: I don't think politics is the only factor. The intifada has typically involved everyone — the old people, the young girls, everybody. In the villages in the Ramallah area, one cannot say that the left-wing forces are strong, yet women have had a very active role. In more than one village, women have been killed. Simple self-defense in facing a present threat is involved. If they come to my house or the house of my neighbor or if they take someone, then I must go out to help. If there are settlers, I must go out and throw stones.

Another factor is that the one who works and brings home an income is the one who makes decisions. Why is the woman enslaved — or at least not liberated? It is because she is kept at home. I have seen women who have gone out to work become the decision makers at home. In the intifada too, the one who works makes decisions. The woman who takes to the street at the time of demonstrations and sees others participating will also become a part. You can see that even the religious women become a part; if you ask them whether the army is in the area, they will answer.

Things take a long time to change. In our camp you can see men and women active together on the street. Maybe in Hebron you will not see this, but even there it is not like it was. There have been changes. Before the intifada, a woman might have feared leaving her house, but now she often goes out to work in the national institutions, in the women's committees. Sometimes she goes out to teach small groups of ten or fifteen children. She has now the ability to make her own decisions, and sometimes she does not tell her father the truth. Not everything I tell my father is the truth. She has her own ideas, and she sticks to them.

Hassan: This is something we have in common with all of Arab society, whether in Jordan or in Syria. Religion has had a great role for fourteen hundred years. It has a great influence on Oriental society. There is no way that the intifada in two years can remove all these obstacles in the path of women. We cannot quickly divest ourselves of these customs and traditions that have been around for hundreds of years. Before the intifada, our camp had women who worked and were active in various social committees. During the intifada this has grown, and now the woman's role is greater. Sometimes there are even more women than men in the demonstrations. All the girls take to the streets with the young men. If one girl sees another taking to the streets, then the next day she too will join.

Umar: I agree that we live in a society that is dominated by traditions and customs, but the intifada has helped a lot in focusing on the woman's role nationally. We often see women participating in demonstrations, working in work committees or in the kindergartens, which did not happen twenty or thirty years ago.

The role of the woman throughout the world has developed, which influences women here. They say, "Why should we not be like a woman in America or in Europe?" The strengthening of the woman has led her to make her own decisions. The father or brother in the family now seeks her advice, and she goes to university, something unheard of before. She is consulted on her marriage. The woman has begun to play her role in society just like a woman anywhere else.

Ali: Some years ago if a girl went out and threw a stone, the old people would say she was immoral, but today it is a regular thing. It is like styles of fashion. You get used to it. It has become normal for girls to participate, to talk to the young men.

Eds.: Who will rule Palestine once the Occupation ends?

Hassan: The Palestinian people are struggling for a popular democratic state — nothing more and nothing less. In this state there will be full rights so that I can choose the president. If someone wants to be the president of the Palestinian people without their agreement, the people will reject that person. They will say: "Get down! We have built the state, and it is our right to choose the president." The nation will decide whether it wants notables like the Nashashibis or the Husaynis. Maybe I will choose someone from the refugee camps to be the president. I might feel that such a person has done much more to further the cause than someone who witnessed the struggle from a distance. Someone who has spent ten or fifteen years in prison has more of a right to lead than the person who has done nothing. If the notables rule, then I do not want a state. If the state is a dictatorship, then I want nothing to do with it.

Ali: All these notables are entrepreneurs. They have a vested interest in the Occupation. There is no possibility that they would strive for Palestinian interests. If they did strive for these interests, then the Occupation would not have chosen them.

The PLO knows very well that the Palestinians in the Occupied Territories have their own point of view. Freij, for example, once suggested the idea of a period of calm during the intifada and then saw the reaction of the people in the street concerning his proclamation. The PLO threatened to kill him. But perhaps the PLO suggested the plan and asked him to announce it. Possibly they wanted to test the reaction on the street.

Hassan: During the intifada these notables have increased in number, and they have talked a lot about the position of the future state concerning various issues. These reactionary notables who emerged before and during the intifada are not accepted by 95 percent of the Palestinian people. They know that these personalities do not have our interests at heart. These personalities do not live the life we live; their lives are not in a single room in a refugee camp. They do not live on the same level. They are not a part of the people who are suffering intense injustice. Their role is in fact a negative one, since they try to stop the intifada instead of pushing it forward.

Ali: In any disagreement between the masses of the people and the leadership, it is the people who must choose those who are to have the responsibility of leadership. The right wing, however, is self-interested.

Umar: Here, on the street, everyone supports a different group — Fatah, the Popular Front, and so forth. But one thing is clear: the people are exasperated. The working people, the poor, and the people in the refugee camps are certain about continuing the intifada, continuing the struggle.

Uthman: The problem is that the PLO outside is quite happy with these personalities. Most of these personalities were chosen by the PLO itself. There is a gap between the masses of the people here, who reject these personalities, and the PLO, which might have even accepted the election plan. The PLO is compromising its principles bit by bit without any guarantees, and we reject this logic.

The PLO is a term for various groups, including Fatah, the Popular Front for the Liberation of Palestine, the Palestinian Communist Party, the Democratic Front, and the Struggle Front. Then there are also groups outside the PLO, such as those aligned with Abu Musa. Inside the PLO different groups struggle for power. There is the radical left force and what we call the opportunist left. Then there is the right wing, which is the ruling force today.

The right is composed of bourgeois groups, and in any revolution these groups are progressively willing to renounce more and more. They typically compromise their principles. In the beginning the voice of the intifada supported the right wing, but as it compromised, the intifada retreated. This right wing is willing to renounce more than the intifada could gain. The right tries to impose its will on all. They changed the national covenant, and their opinion as concerns the elections was also a renunciation of principles. The front said no to the elections because nothing could be gained by them.

Some groups in the PLO are willing to compromise with the right wing to preserve the unity of the PLO. The Popular Front, for example, surprised everyone on the street by being willing to accept UN Resolution 242, although it meant nothing for the people. The entire struggle and strategy of the Popular Front were against 242, but at the same time they were following the principle of staying within the PLO, and therefore compromise was necessary. Every group that leaves the PLO is a loss for us, and it weakens the intifada. If they left, there would have been three PLOs instead of one. We already have the Salvation Front outside the PLO, composed of Abu Musa, Saiqa, Ahmad Jibril, and others. So we would have had three PLOs.

We would love to have elections, even if it's just for the sake of a celebration. We need to ask, however, what the people would gain from it all. That is the simple question. Ask the old people in their seventies and eighties what they think of the elections, and they reply, "Will it give us a state?" If you say no, then they say, "No, we don't want elections then."

Eytan and Noam

On the Israeli side, those facing the Palestinian shabab at the front have been young men serving in the Israeli Defense Forces. For over twenty years these young men have patrolled the Occupied Territories, their task being to keep order, prevent disturbances, and enable the smooth continuation of Occupation. Their task has never been so difficult as during the period of the intifada. These soldiers, trained in one of the most efficient and modern armies in the world, have proved their military prowess in the succession of wars Israel has fought against its Arab neighbors since 1948. Now faced with a civil uprising and a largely unarmed civilian population, these young men find themselves at their most vulnerable. The Israeli army has had to deal with desertion, insubordination, and conscientious objection on a large scale. Widespread accusations of brutality have led, in some cases, to showcase military trials.

We spoke with Eytan (twenty-four years old) and Noam (twenty-three), two young men who serve in the military reserves as Israeli soldiers in the occupied West Bank.

Editors: How has the intifada helped to clarify the issue of justice in the Israeli-Palestinian conflict?

Noam: In general I do not think that it has helped to clarify anything. From my point of view it has only complicated matters. That is not to say that now I have answers. I don't. Although the problem is very transparent, I cannot say anything specific about where exactly the injustice lies, whether on this side or that. I cannot say that on this or that specific point matters must be dealt with. The intifada leaves me quite up in the air.

Before the intifada I was less aware, and possibly it was all less problematic. The very fact that the intifada is taking place, that things are happening out there, pushes the issue into consciousness. Now one has to dedicate more time to thinking about it, asking why matters have reached this point. I do not have any solutions, but my consciousness is greater.

Eytan: I think that the intifada definitely raised the level of consciousness among Israelis concerning the situation. I can recall a cousin of mine who lives on a moshav near Netanya saying: "Why can't things stay the way they are? They will live there; I will live here. I don't need this type of pain in the butt — it's not good for me, and it's not good for them." But the intifada has brought things to the surface. It has brought the whole situation to a stage where almost everyone agrees that some sort of solution has to be reached. One cannot just let things continue the way they are, or let them simmer until they reach the boiling point.

Eds.: Why do you think the Palestinians initiated the intifada?

Noam: That's a good question. Well, it is clear that there has been a crystallization of more nationalist thinking. There is an increased desire for independence. There is a tendency toward separatism: Palestinians see themselves as Palestinians and not as Israeli citizens living in Israel.

Why did this start now, twenty years after the Israeli Occupation? It is difficult to say. I have only the impressions from the news media and from my relatively minimal experience in the field during my reserve duty.

I served in the area of Tulkarm for a very short period. The experience was a very difficult one, with great psychological pressure. One goes to reserve duty, and in the future I will continue to go to reserve duty. But this work is very unpleasant. In dealing with the population, you can actually feel the sense of rebellion in the intifada. There is incitement everywhere. You, wearing a uniform, represent the Israeli side, and they, on the other side, represent the Palestinian side.

Principally my goal as a soldier on arriving in the area is to maintain order. Generally this refers specifically to the thoroughfares that pass through the region. This work.involves violence, which makes it unpleasant. I was not violent in this period, but the work itself deals with violence. When you're in the area, you have to respond to the fact that stones have been thrown or that they have raised some kind of roadblock or that they have written slogans on the walls. You have to respond to this, and generally you try to make sure that the response will not be violent. You try not to use violence against violence.

It is difficult, and psychological pressure is exerted on you. When you are attacked — and you are constantly attacked out there — you tend to get angry because they try to harm you, and they sometimes succeed. Everyday you get hit by stones on every part of your body. It is natural that when they hit you, you want to hit back. But in my own experience and from the things I saw in the field, it does not work like that. You have to respond, but it has to be in a different currency because you are the force that has to preserve order in the area. It is psychologically difficult to stand up to this. You are split most of the time. On the one hand you understand the need for restraint, yet on the other hand you are angry.

Eytan: You asked, "Why did the Palestinians make an intifada?" I do not pose questions like that. When we are brought into the territories to do our military service, our mission is simply to keep the roads clear and the passage safe for any passengers or transportation passing through, whether it be Arab or Israeli. That is necessary mainly where there are Israeli settlements. If there is a military base, that means the road must be kept clear. If there is a small Israeli village and the school bus has to take the children of the village to the area school, then that road has to be kept clear. This was the case in the village I served in — Yaabad, near Jenin. A cliff overlooks the road there. Whenever a school bus passes, rocks and bottles are thrown from the cliff onto the bus. Our job is to keep the peace and keep the roads open.

In short, I do not bother myself with issues of why they think the way they think. I am more concerned about us and me. Why am I doing this? Why do I have to act a certain way? How does this all affect me and my friends? As an Israeli, how does this affect Israelis and Jews? The question of what happens to the Arab kid who gets beaten up is less of an issue for me. Not that I want the kid to be beaten up or shot, but why did the Israeli soldier have to beat him or use arms? What brought the Israeli to this situation? How does it affect him, and how does it affect me as an Israeli? That is what bothers me.

Now, as Noam said, you're put in a situation you didn't ask to be in. I, like Noam, will not refuse to do army service. If anyone in my unit would refuse for political reasons, I would not want him back in my unit. I would not be able to trust that person in a situation where I have to trust him with my life. That is the bottom line in any army where you are serving alongside other soldiers and you are in a situation of life and death. You have to trust your companion completely.

I know from personal experience that the intifada is hard; it can get very emotional and places soldiers in a lot of stress. After two years of trying to deal with it, it is still not quite clear what you are supposed to do. Let us say that a Molotov cocktail is thrown at you. A Molotov cocktail is quite a lethal weapon — maybe not as lethal as a bullet to the heart, but it is still quite capable of inflicting serious injury, even death. If it is in the air, on its way, and you identify the person who threw it, you can shoot to kill. Once it has landed and exploded — it makes no difference if anybody is injured — you cannot shoot to kill. Those are the orders. Some military psychologists and public relations people asked us: "You know these are the orders. How would you react? What would you do?" The majority of the guys said: "If it lands and explodes, I will still shoot to kill. If someone tries to kill me, I am not going to say, 'Well, if I had seen it one second before it landed, then I will make all these distinctions.'"

When you are on patrol with three or four other soldiers and you are mobbed, how can you start thinking clearly and calmly? Well, chapter 1, paragraph 8, says that in this type of situation the orders are that I must do *a, b, c,* and *d*. You simply are not likely to act like this in a terrifying situation. You cannot think clearly and act calmly and go by what the book says. A lot of soldiers get screwed because they reacted on the spur of the moment, when they felt that their lives were in danger in a particular situation. But a television camera on the side did not see it that way, or the military tribunal did not see it that way, or the press did not see it that way. Outsiders cannot look into the mind of that soldier and see what he saw.

Eds.: There have been highly publicized trials of soldiers who were sentenced for brutality in putting down the intifada. What do you think about these trials, or about the idea that a soldier is responsible only to obey orders?

Eytan: Once we were ordered to commandeer civilian vehicles. We were told to stop cars, to tell the people driving to step out and inform them that they would receive their automobiles the following day. These were cars belonging to Palestinian Arabs with blue plates. To put it mildly, I was very annoyed by this order. We were discussing it among ourselves — right wing, left wing, and centrists — and we all agreed that this was something that should not be done. According to proper procedure, something like this, which is not a matter of life and death, is illegal. But first you must proceed to obey the order, and then you can ask questions or complain. I was fairly vocal. Afterward I was told that almost everyone in the unit was not happy with the order given. We obeyed it though; we commandeered the number of vehicles required.

I personally approach these issues with the consciousness that I am a soldier and that a soldier's job is to obey orders. Whether I agree with the particular order or feel comfortable with it doesn't matter — unless it is really out of the ordinary and truly unacceptable. For example, if someone ordered me to break bones, I would not do so. If someone ordered me to beat someone up after I had captured that person, I would not do so. If someone told me to shoot to kill a person who was not fleeing or had not taken part in an act of violence, I would not do so. I think that in my particular unit the majority of soldiers agree with my point of view, and they keep the minority, who are more violent and more outspokenly right wing, in check.

Eds.: Let's get back to the question of what you think gave rise to the intifada?

Eytan: You are talking about twenty years of Occupation, about relegating people to being second- or third-class citizens. You are asking why the Palestinian issue is so big in the press. A lot of soldiers speak out and say: "Why does everyone have to look at us with a microscope and dissect every action and photograph everything that is happening? Minorities all over the world are subjected to inhumane conditions. Violence is prevalent in other societies, yet it is not written on the front page of the newspaper. Why are our moral standards supposed to be higher than those of the rest of the world?"

Why the uprising? A lot of it is politics, a lot of it is press. A lot of people who would acquiesce to a situation, whether good or bad, are told that their situation is not a healthy one. The point is made over and over again. I think that is one of the main causes. I do not think that the conditions in the West Bank are inhumane compared with other parts of the world. I do not think that the standard of living is so terrible that there is no way out other than the intifada. I did see poverty like I had never seen. There is a great difference between Baqa al-Gharbiyyah and Baqa al-Sharqiyyah, two places that are a five-minute walk from each other. One is beyond the Green Line, and one is inside the Green Line. You see the difference in the standard of living, in car models, in houses, in the wares in the shops, and in the clothes people wear.

Noam: I quite agree with Eytan. The situation is quite clear. The Occupation was established twenty years ago. I think there are basic differences in mentality and way of life. The Israeli tendency is to look to the West, and the Arab tendency is to hold on to Arab culture, which has Oriental characteristics. Right here is the root of the problem: there is a cultural gap, a difference in how the world is perceived. It seems to me that this is the basis of everything. If there was less of a difference from a cultural point of view, then it might be easier. Maybe the intifada would not have broken out. Do not misunderstand me — I am not negating Arab culture; each culture has its positive characteristics and its less positive ones. When two cultures like these confront each other and clash with each other as a result of the situation of Occupation, then you have a problem.

I think it is also true to say that there was a type of specifically political incitement. Their interest was to provoke rebellion here, but this is insufficient to explain it all. This incitement obviously fell on fertile ground, indicating that there was a problem out there. The problem is exceedingly complex. I am not a sociologist and have not researched the problem. I have not spoken to the Arabs and am informed only through the news media, so there are things I do not know.

Eds.: Was there any incident during your reserve duty that led to an instantaneous identification with the other side and a moment of insight that their struggle is a just one?

Eytan: No, there was not.

Noam: There was never a moment when I said to myself, "Hey, they are in the right." This did not happen, but something similar happened. When you are out there, you are within a framework of certain norms. You are the soldier, and you represent the Israeli side and maintain order. You feel, work, and think like a soldier. There is a separation between you and the other side.

Something did happen once that was special — not externally but internally. On patrol duty I got into a discussion once with the locals concerning some matters of procedure. I was talking with a young Arab girl who looked at me a certain way when she spoke to me. They always looked at me as a soldier, as the one maintaining order, and there was hate and provocation in their look. But with her, I could tell that she saw me as a human being. And I felt the same thing. It was very special because suddenly you say to yourself: "Wait a minute. You could easily be my sister or my mother or even my girlfriend." We had communicated on a very deep level just because of one look. From my point of view this did something to me, something very strong. I did not change my mode of behavior, but something changed in my thinking. Suddenly I said to myself, "Hey, in reality we are all the same."

Eytan: Are they justified in some way? I would say that in certain things they are — for instance, concerning the collaborators. We could not understand how these people were still alive. As Israeli soldiers, we had to deal with these collaborators. We had to work alongside these collaborators, and we could not understand how the people in the village did not beat their brains out. That would be justified in my opinion. I would not be able to live next door to someone who is collaborating with my enemy, with the soldiers who are occupying my village. The hatred for them I could understand. I could understand their hatred for me, but in my opinion it was not justified. I personally did not do anything to justify their hatred or their fear of me. We need to get out of the territories, though — not so they can live their lives, but so I can live my life. That would be my reason for getting out of the territories.

Eds.: What do you see as being a just solution?

Eytan: I do not want to deal with the intifada. I do not want to have to go into people's homes where I am not wanted. We must get out of there. There are not so many units that do serve there, and the burden falls on the shoulders of a few. They have to deal with it daily. I do not want to deal with it, whether that means talking to the PLO, or whether it means getting out of most of the territories. I know that there are very strong points to the argument that for security reasons we cannot get out. I do not want to live in the Netanya area, a strip seven kilometers wide, with the fear that Israel can be easily cut in two at this point. I am not willing to live in fear. I am willing to fight, to serve in the army for secure borders so that my family and my friends can live in peace.

Noam: The question of a just solution is the nucleus, and it is the hardest question. I do not think that I have in my head, even intuitively, a formula for a compromise for peace. Yes, I do want peace; I do not want to continue being the "bad" soldier in the West Bank. I want it all to end. That will be good for them, and it will be good for me too. We are talking about a very complex situation, a population made up of so many different groups and factions, so many different opinions, on both sides. It is very difficult to sew this all together. I want to reach such a solution, but I do not have a realistic way to make it better. If it were at all realistic, then we need all the different parties to take one step forward — for example, a step forward of expressing readiness to come together and speak to each other. Maybe even not to speak but rather to understand that the situation is a complex one and there is a need for a solution. This must precede the call to come and talk together.

I don't know what would happen if suddenly the government decided that we are beginning talks with the PLO. What would happen if they did sit down with the PLO and work out some form of territorial compromise under some kind of conditions? I am doubtful whether such a position would in fact silence the intifada. I think that the matter is much larger than this, perhaps a matter of education that must start among us and among them, including more understanding, openness, and taking the other into account — things that are in fact the ABCs of morals and society. I think that if a generation arose on both sides that was educated on this, then a linking up would evolve.

Eytan: Noam's basic idea of a utopian state where our children are brought up to talk understanding and acceptance rather than hatred is nice, but if an Arab girl sees a soldier shooting her brother or sister, or a young boy from Israel sees his brother or sister being blown up in a bus, it is very hard to take these ingrained attitudes and turn them around. It takes a lot of effort, and that is a state of utopia.

Basically you are talking about two peoples who are fighting for one land. In my opinion there is only one way to reach some state of stability, and I am not talking about peace — I am talking about acceptance. I do not want to live with the Palestinians. I will accept living alongside the Palestinians because it will better my life. It will obviously better theirs, but that is not what bothers me. That is not the issue that burns inside me, that they should have a better life. You have to take out the radicalism. Radicalism to the far right and to the far left in both camps is unreasonable. You cannot parley with a radical. You cannot negotiate with a radical. You cannot compromise, but here you have to.

I think that right now the situation is unbearable. To continue with the situation as it is — to live with the intifada for another twenty years — is impossible. This is not life. We must go one step further and say yes, we will talk to the PLO. To say outright no, we will not talk to the PLO because it is a terrorist organization, is unacceptable. Yes, they are my enemies; yes they possibly hate me, and yes I possibly hate them, but I cannot reach any compromise with my enemies without talking to them. If they are my stated enemies, then I must talk to them to reach some form of compromise. To say that we will not get out of any of the Occupied Territories and not allow a Palestinian state is simply repeating the old positions that have been stated for the past forty years and have gotten us nowhere. So we must advance one step further. Whether this will help or not, I do not know, but it is much better then doing nothing.

Farida and Jamila

Standing alongside the young Palestinian men in the struggle against Occupation are the young women. They are caught between two societies — the traditional society of their parents, which has confined women to specific roles, and the modernizing society, which is changing rapidly, accelerated because of the intifada. These young women are willing to pay the price for their involvement in the struggle for national liberation, and many have been killed, wounded, or imprisoned. Yet alongside their struggle for national liberation, they are working for change within Palestinian society too.

We spoke with Farida (seventeen years old) and Jamila (nineteen), two residents of a Palestinian refugee camp on the West Bank.

Editors: How has the intifada clarified issues of justice in the Israeli-Palestinian struggle?

Farida: At the time that the intifada broke out, it became the subject that everyone discussed throughout the world. It gave people the opportunity to see the cruelty and violence that the Israelis have practiced against the Palestinians.

Jamila: When Israel occupied the Palestinian lands in 1967, it tried to show the rest of the world that the Palestinians were terrorists. It tried to show that this land is the Land of Israel and that Israel has suffered injustice. It hid what it was doing against the Palestinians and presented itself as the protector of Palestinian rights here. The intifada burst out as a result of things that had happened, not just over a day or a month or even a year, but over twenty years of Occupation in the West Bank and the Gaza Strip. The intifada revealed Israel's true face. As a result of seeing the intifada and the methods of Israeli repression, world opinion toward Israel began to change.

Farida: The intifada also clarified the situation to Palestinians, some of whom had been relatively untouched by the Occupation. The intifada clarified to Palestinians inside Palestine and to those in the Diaspora exactly how the Palestinian people are suffering under Occupation. As a result of the intifada, those people who did not think seriously about the problem were forced to reconsider. Now it is not just a few fighters who are struggling to defend the rights of the people; rather, the struggle has spread to all the people.

Eds.: What can you do to assist your people in reaching a just solution?

Farida: Our aim is a Palestinian state, which we have a right to, since it is our land. Those Jews who are coming have no right to a state here. They do have a right to live in dignity in whichever country they choose, but they have no right to violate the rights of others. Let them come and live here with us, but we should be the rulers. The only way we can fight the possibility of increasing immigration from the Soviet Union is to increase the intifada and bring more pressure to bear on Israel. When the intifada broke out, one of its central goals was the creation of an independent Palestinian state. The intifada serves as the beginning of our struggle and not as the end. The intifada is the first of perhaps many stations on the way, many methods of struggle.

Jamila: Before the intifada when we did something concerning our problem, many people did not accept it, whether in the camps or throughout the region; we were only a small group. Now, in the shadow of the intifada, whatever we do is greeted by great enthusiasm by the residents. Our first goal is a state in the Occupied Territories of 1967 — the West Bank and the Gaza Strip. This is our first goal, and after we establish a state there and build it up, we can deal with the problem of our lands from 1948, Jaffa and the other areas.

The Jews say that this is the State of Israel, but this is incorrect. We might be able to live with the Jews in that area, but then they would need to be just like the Christians who live among us. They would be nationalists, just like the Christians, and they would have all the rights — the right to their religion, their language, their names — but all this under the rule of the Palestinian state. The government will be secular, and Muslims, Christians, and Jews will all live as Palestinians.

Eds.: How can this be realized?

Farida: The only way is through struggle.

Jamila: The intifada is one step in the struggle. After the intifada, which remains on the level of stone throwing, comes the armed revolution. This armed revolution will bring about the independent state. But after the establishment of that state, the question remains how we will live with Israel. If we have a democratic government in the Palestinian state, then we might be able to reach an agreement with Israel and the Jews as regards the inclusion of Israel within the democratic Palestinian state.

The intifada and the stone throwing have brought many results, but these things will not become reality just through the stone throwing. Rather, what is necessary is that the intifada progress and become a real revolution. One cannot use only stones in a revolution; one must use arms. Otherwise how are we going to wrest our concessions from Israel? The Palestinian state exists now on paper as a result of the intifada, but we can make it a reality only through armed struggle.

Farida: The stone throwing and the intifada have clarified to the world that we are suffering injustice, that Israel is the real extremist — but it has not brought a solution. Sure, many countries now agree that we are justified, and they say they support us, but what are they doing in reality? Nothing. There has to be another stage that involves small armed groups undertaking military actions against the army and other targets. We are not talking here about two armies facing each other, an Israeli one and a Palestinian one.

Jamila: We are certainly not talking here about conventional war like the world wars. The Palestinian revolution will be carried out by small armed groups who will carry out military actions against Israeli targets. We have no way of winning a conventional war against the Israelis, because they have much more military equipment at their disposal than we have.

Eds.: How has the intifada affected the young women?

Farida: The intifada has helped a great deal in the struggle to achieve equality. Before the intifada very few women actively participated in the struggle, whether throwing stones or planting explosives. Now any woman, young or old, goes out to participate. The intifada has entered every house, every area, and become a regular way of life. Women are now permitted to participate in this struggle. Before the intifada there was some development, and sometimes women did participate in spontaneous activities, like stone throwing. Women are now completely ready to participate in military activities just like the young men. The situation is still not perfect; the role of women has improved, but not in all spheres.

Jamila: There is even the possibility that after the intifada women will regress to their status before the intifada. As Farida said, before the intifada there were some developments that provided a framework for this struggle to attain equality. These frameworks assist women to reach a consciousness that will prevent a return to the past, before the intifada. We have seen what happened in places like Algeria. That teaches us that the women must secure their status during the intifada so that they do not go backward after the revolution.

Eds.: What will you do if the men say, after the intifada, "Well, thank you very much, but now you must return to the kitchen"?

Farida: It is not possible that they would say this because they have already let their wives, sisters, and daughters out of the house. How is the man going to change his mind afterward? Anyway, the woman is going to be much more developed, and her personality will be stronger; she will not agree. She will have a better idea of what her rights are.

Jamila: We have indeed reached a great degree of consciousness, both young men and women, but this does not mean to say it will be sustained after the revolution. The fear is a very real one that these same young men will try to return us to the confines of the home after the revolution. For that very reason women have to continue to struggle to become more and more conscious in order to affirm their rights.

Farida: But these young men know now that the role of the woman goes beyond the kitchen or the confines of the home. The intifada has made clear what the woman is capable of and how important her role is. They too have become conscious that there are few spheres that are solely for men.

Jamila: Women now leave the home to visit the wounded, visit the families of martyrs, participate in special women's demonstrations, or, together with the young men, keep the strikes. Before the intifada there was very little of this, but now it has increased greatly.

Farida: These are all developments on the political level, but there have also been some changes on the social level. The personality of the woman has grown much stronger, and she now has the forcefulness to stand up to her father and maybe even refuse the man that has been chosen for her to marry.

Eds.: What are you doing to make those around you more aware?

Farida: We participate wherever we can, particularly in the women's committees. These activities include the usual kinds of solidarity visits to the wounded and to the families of martyrs and detainees. We help the needy and also have political discussions.

Jamila: These women's frameworks are a way of transmitting the Palestinian point of view to the people. Many people are ignorant of the Palestinian viewpoint, since their only source of information is the news. We attempt to clarify what the Palestinians believe and what they are aiming at and what is happening in the greater arena. We are working here in the camp, but these frameworks exist everywhere — in the cities, the villages, and other camps.

Eds.: What made you aware of the injustice in the situation?

Jamila: My own particular situation involving my family and my environment has made me aware. We are living in a camp, and it is here that the Occupation is most evident, maybe more so than in towns like Bethlehem. Here we have had arrests long before the intifada, including even brothers who were detained. This is enough to make us more aware than those in Bethlehem who have businesses, who live in comfort and make a profit. They send their children to the best schools and then overseas to continue their education. The Occupation has scarcely affected them at all. The Palestinian problem for them is nothing more than something in the news or something brought up at various conferences.

Farida: These people do not even have any interest in changing the situation; it is we who want to change. There are even people in the camps who are not aware, selfish people who love only themselves. But as for me, from the day I came into the world, I understood. It was enough just to see the army and what it is doing in the camp. I understood that I must try to get back my rights and the rights of my people.

Benny Katzover

Perched on a spectacular hilltop overlooking the West Bank city of Nablus is the little Jewish settlement of Eilon Moreh, one of more than 120 Israeli settlements that are spread throughout the occupied West Bank, Gaza Strip, and Golan Heights. The residents of these settlements regard the Occupied Territories as home, an indivisible part of the biblical Land of Israel, promised by God to the People of Israel. As far as they are concerned, the intifada is no different from the other wars that Israel has fought against the Arabs, who, according to them, reject any notion of Jewish sovereignty in the area. These settlers insist on making their presence felt. They patrol the Occupied Territories heavily armed and often are involved in violent clashes with Palestinians. Their mixture of religion and nationalism has widespread appeal in Israel.

We spoke with Benny Katzover, head of the Samaria Regional Council in his office in Eilon Moreh. Mr. Katzover is a founder of Gush Emunim (Bloc of the Faithful), a popular movement that supports Jewish settlement in, and sovereignty over, the Occupied Territories. He is also an active member in the Tehiya (Rebirth) party, a right-wing Knesset faction.

Editors: How do you understand the concept of justice in the context of the Israeli-Arab conflict, and how can one reach a just solution to this conflict?

Benny: In no conflict in the world is the justice of one side so apparent as that of the Israelis. I say this without apology and without hesitation. There are two levels to this: the historical level and the realistic level. There is no meaning to the concept "Land of Israel" or "the Holy Land" except in connection with the Jewish people. Where does the world get Jerusalem from? Where does the world get Shechem (Nablus) or Hebron from? Historical justice can only mean giving the Jewish people its little corner — and it is indeed a little corner — both within the context of the Middle East and within the context of the whole world.

Concerning the Israeli-Arab conflict, not only are there twenty-two Arab countries, but they also stretch over millions of square kilometers, whereas we are talking of a Land of Israel only twenty-eight thousand square kilometers in size. This is a strip of land that, until 1948, was never sovereign. It was always conquered territory, under Crusader and, later, Turkish and British rule. Until we returned here, this strip did not belong, in a sovereign sense, to any other people. Some people utterly confuse the right of an individual to live in a certain place and that individual's claim to sovereignty. I see nothing more just than the fact that the Land of Israel belongs to the people of Israel.

Moreover, this is strengthened when one adds the practical aspect, the simple reality of the present. The Land of Israel, according to both Jews and Palestinians, referred historically to both banks of the Jordan River. When the British decided to take between 70 and 80 percent of this land and give it to King Hussein's grandfather, we were forced to accept this. Thereby three-quarters of the Land of Israel passed out of our control and became the Hashemite Kingdom in Transjordan. We remained silent. When the United Nations requisitioned another half of what remained to give the Arabs half and us half, again we kept silent. We agreed.

But the other side tried to break our hold over the Land of Israel, from the beginning of the Zionist movement and even before that. They did not accept the UN resolution regarding partition and declared war. We succeeded in liberating a quarter of the land because they had declared war. In 1967 they initiated another round of war and again tried to destroy us. Instead of them destroying us, we liberated another quarter of the Land of Israel. How can they now come with any claims? We agreed to the compromises, and they rejected them. Once they tried to destroy us, then a second time they tried to destroy us, and now what obligation do we have to them? After all, this is the Land of Israel — we agreed to compromise, and they did not. They did not even make known their disagreement in the spirit of two neighbors fighting over a house and taking it to court; they simply tried to destroy us.

There never was Palestinian sovereignty here. When this strip of land was ruled for nineteen years by King Hussein, nobody claimed that a Palestinian state should be set up in Judea and Samaria. Not one single Arab country talked of establishing a Palestinian state in Judea and Samaria. Not even the Palestinians themselves talked about the establishment of a Palestinian state in Judea and Samaria. If the territory was ruled by Hussein, it was okay. Back then they spoke about a Palestinian state in Tel Aviv, at least until 1967. They talked about the 1948 borders, the last outpost of Zionism. Now, during the intifada, again they have decided to fight.

We always treated them with consideration. Those who were in Israel before 1967 were granted almost total equal rights. We did not treat them as the enemy, although they are in fact enemies and behave as such. After 1967, everything we enjoyed in the State of Israel we bestowed on the Palestinians in Judea and Samaria, including frameworks of health, economy, society, and education. During Hussein's time, however, they did not have a single newspaper or a single university.

We were under the illusion that we could live together. Now they have decided that they do not want to live with us. This is the clear decision of the intifada. I fear that they are about to bring upon themselves another disaster, like the one they brought upon themselves in 1948. But the decision is theirs. We provided the best conditions for them, and they kicked us in return. They have constantly tried to harm us. They have tried to expel us, and in the end, I think, they will crumble.

Eds.: What would you do if, because of the intifada, a Palestinian state is established in Judea, Samaria, and Gaza?

Benny: It will never be established. It cannot be established. This is like an egg that you have made into an omelette — you cannot make it into an egg again. No government in Israel, or anyone else, can simply remove the 100,000 Jews who live in Judea and Samaria, the 120,000 Jews in East Jerusalem, or the 120 Jewish settlements. This is all something alive in the soul of at least 50 to 60 percent of the Jewish population in Israel. If there had been talk of this back in 1968 or 1969, then maybe there would have been something to talk about, but for a long time there has not been anything to talk about.

Eds.: How can you convince the Palestinian residents of these territories that this is the reality and that they might as well stop talking about a Palestinian state?

Benny: Three things. First, the Jewish presence here must be greatly strengthened. This is the most important thing, as it will clarify the situation to them better than anything else. Second, we need a much more viable Israeli policy. And the third thing is annexation, the extension of Israeli law and sovereignty to those areas. While they see us hesitating, stammering, stuttering, and arguing among ourselves, they are full of illusions. Just as they have no illusions about Tel Aviv or Haifa, they should not have illusions about Judea and Samaria.

Unfortunately there is a segment of the Israeli public that still does not understand the intensity of our connection to this area, historically and daily. They will understand eventually, and that connection is growing daily. We are one hundred thousand Jews here; the overwhelming majority having arrived in the last ten years. This is already 80 percent sovereignty, and any annexation is actually not very important. The return home, the growth, the development of the connection is the main thing, and that is developing grandly. We travel up and down here day and night. Almost on every main road there is vibrant Jewish life. This is getting stronger and stronger. This is, in fact, developing much faster than in any other chapter of Zionist history.

Sooner or later they are simply not going to have an alternative, and they are going to have to come to terms with the reality. Either they will come to terms with it, or they will continue the struggle, but in that struggle only they will crumble. This will be the third round of a disaster they bring upon themselves. Today we have thirty-seven settlements in this area; at the beginning of the intifada we had thirty-two or thirty-three. Formerly, 100 percent of all these settlements had excellent neighborly relations with the Arab villages around them. This was expressed in mutual visits, mutual assistance, and participation in each other's celebrations — they would come to our house warmings, and we would go to theirs. We would assist them with the authorities, show them how to establish kindergartens or workshops. Those among us opposing coexistence with them constituted only 3 or 4 percent of the settler population.

But they killed our children and women and men also. Every day they try to harm our children as they return from school. This all has a price. Now the Jewish population who lives here has had enough and no longer believes in the possibility of peaceful coexistence with them. They have decided to continue their struggle against us. In the past the population believed that Israeli law should be extended to Judea and Samaria and that the Arabs should be given full rights, but today very few believe this. Today the vast majority believes that we would be crazy to allow them to be part of the decision-making process in our Jewish state because they have proved, beyond a shadow of doubt, that all they want is to destroy us. In the old days there were a lot of people who trusted them, who were naive enough to suggest doing business with them, believing that they were people like everyone else. Today the message is clear: they are our enemies. They are simply waiting for the first opportunity to stick a knife into us. Whoever continues to fight us will be fought to the bitter end; whoever wants to live here in peace will be allowed to do so, although they will not have the vote. They will enjoy all other rights — basic human rights and freedom of universities, press, and opinion. No one will harm them. They will be like those people who apply for American citizenship but do not fulfil all the requirements and therefore can live there but without citizenship.

Eds.: What role do you play in all this?

Benny: I am the head of the Samaria Regional Council, in which we have thirty-three settlements. In my area we have fourteen thousand residents. Alongside us here in Samaria we have four independent councils, which include another fourteen thousand residents. About half are religious, and half are secular. Our aim all along was to turn this into just an ordinary residential area, attracting the public at large. Thank God, today we are succeeding. Those coming are attracted by various things. In the beginning ideological people came, but if I want to bring tens of thousands and not a few individuals, I have to improve the standard of living. People understand today that it is comfortable to live here. The quality of life offered is very special, on all levels. The feeling of individuals who live here is that they are not simply nuts or bolts in the city but rather their life has meaning, even if they are not religious. They feel that they influence their community, fashion it and determine its future.

Eds.: Aren't these people afraid? How can they endure attacks and endanger their children, even for matters of principle?

Benny: I did say that our children are attacked, but I did not say that they are in mortal danger. All in all, the danger here is not higher than anywhere else. In Jerusalem there have been even more terrorist incidents; does that mean we will not live in Jerusalem? In Wadi 'Ara and in Galilee there is also danger, although this is not publicized. The Jewish people as a rule have never been cowards. The stages we have passed through already were more dangerous and more problematic than the intifada. Look at what Zionism went through during the 1929 and 1936 riots, when they were the strong ones and we were weak, or during the period of the feda'in, when everyone throughout Israel was in danger. The level of danger is simply different today.

Overseas they make the mistake of thinking that there is constant war here and you simply cannot walk on the street. This is not correct. They think this even more so about Judea and Samaria, and sometimes even the Israelis in Tel Aviv think this, but it is simply not true. The fact is that people live here, they go to the movies, they go on picnics, they travel around during the day and night. You do not need any special courage. When there is a more concerted effort to get rid of us, this actually leads to a renewed determination to stay here. Those here say: "What! Now that we are attacked, are we going to leave? Never! We will simply bring more people." It has an inverse effect. Almost every family here who considers whether it is better here or better in Tel Aviv reached the conclusion that it is better here.

Eds.: Is it part of your job to persuade people to stay here, despite the events of the last two years?

Benny: Samaria began to be settled by Jews in 1976. Until the end of 1984 the number of Jews coming here was very small. The overwhelming majority arrived in the last six years. Every year there are a few people who leave because they are not absorbed into the society for social or economic reasons. But during the intifada relatively fewer people have left us than in previous years; the number of those leaving now can be counted on one hand. I am surprised by this. I feared that because of the intifada the percentage of those leaving would grow, but fewer left us during the intifada than at any other period. The growth is greater this year than in the past four years. In fact, we hoped to absorb new immigrants here, but all the houses were taken during the last summer. I would wish that every area in the Land of Israel — the Negev, Galilee, the Jordan Valley, the Golan — would have the success we have had.

Eds.: How do you relate to the claim that you are destroying the Jewish character of the state by insisting on settling areas that are heavily populated with Arabs?

Benny: The people who usually argue this are people whose own Jewish character is very weak. At almost every other period our situation was worse. When Zionism began, there were only a few thousand Jews versus hundreds of thousands of Arabs. Ben-Gurion proclaimed a Jewish state within the partition boundaries, without Ramle, Lyda, Western Galilee, or East Jerusalem. Within these boundaries the Jews were only 52 percent, as opposed to 48 percent Arabs. He was not afraid. The population balance improved afterward with the War of Independence because they were driven out. Immediately after the 1967 war, the population stood at 64 percent Jews and 36 percent Arabs. During the last twenty-three years they have been harping on the same point: "What is going to happen to the Jewish-Arab population balance?" But over the past twenty-three years, the balance has changed only by 1 1/4 percent in favor of the Arabs. Every Jew believes that all kinds of things can happen: the Jewish birth rate can increase, Jewish immigration can flourish. My opponents in the Labour party and in the citizens' rights movement laughed at my optimism, but look at what has happened: the Soviet Jews are coming, and tomorrow there might be immigration here from South Africa.

I never liked the slogan that says, Let's expel the Arabs so we can solve the demographic problem. On principle, I never had any interest in expelling them; rather, I wanted to live with them on good terms. What difference does it make whether they are 30 percent or 60 percent? The character of the state is determined by strength, Jewish education and tradition. Those who are supposedly so concerned with the Jewish character never bothered to encourage immigration. We cannot encourage immigration by giving Jewish immigrants a villa or a Volvo; we cannot compete with America in this. But we can compete in offering the Jews a country with a Jewish character. With all due respect to democracy, and I do not think there is a regime that can replace it, we cannot attract Jews because of our democracy. The democratic regimes in Britain, France, and the United States are a lot more successful.

I was never concerned about the Jewish character of the state, but unfortunately the character of some Jews, who have adopted all kinds of cosmopolitan ideas, is very weak. They deal less and less with their own identity and thereby are weakened. They have also lost all perspective regarding the Arab population. I can understand those who know nothing saying we are conquerors and oppressors, that we should apologize for being here — despite the fact that only yesterday the Arabs wanted to kill us. We have to apologize that our soldiers beat them when they want to harm us. The Arabs who, only yesterday, wanted to stick a knife into me are forgotten, and now they are the victims. When the Arabs were quiet, there was no talk of occupation or oppression, and they enjoyed prosperity.

Eds.: Have you always seen issues in this way?

Benny: Yes. I was educated in a religious school of the religious Zionist movement (Bnei Akiva). Then I went through a religious seminary (Merkaz HaRav), followed by my military service. One year after the Six-Day War, Jewish settlement was established in Hebron. We began there because, historically, Judea is more prominent than Samaria and had a vibrant Jewish community until 1929. It also had the religious sites like the Tomb of the Patriarchs. First I came as a student to help in guard duty, and then I joined. At that first stage, we were a small group of about thirty families.

At a certain point two of us decided to fight for our right to settle in Samaria. One of our chief supporters then was Shimon Peres, who issued an impassioned call to the public, saying that it is absurd that Samaria would be the only place in the world where Jews could not settle. We engaged in a struggle against the government lasting two years, when Rabin was prime minister. We finally established a small group to settle Eilon Moreh in 1973. We settled on the land and were removed by the authorities eight times. Finally we were given a place.

Around this struggle Gush Emunim began. It is a popular movement, supported by tens of thousands. It caused a change in the Zionist direction of the state, giving continuity to the Zionist movement. Veterans of the independence struggle of 1948 flocked to our banner, together with the religious public. Dozens of settlement groups were established, and they created the 120 settlements that we have today in Judea and Samaria. We created the infrastructure for settling one million Jews there — maybe more. The movement is apolitical, and I personally belong to the Tehiya party. The movement is active in many spheres. I think it is the group that can mobilize the biggest number of people to demonstrate on the street in Israel today. It is also the only movement that succeeds in settling large numbers of people in new settlements. The older, established settlement movements, like those of the Labour party, barely manage to establish a settlement every two years. This year we established eight settlements.

Eds.: Have you ever met an educated Arab who has convinced you that there is some degree of justice on the other side?

Benny: I have met Arab intellectuals, but I do not need them to know what the Arabs think. I have had open discussions with village headmen and mayors of the villages and towns in the area. I know exactly what they think and what they want. I have met those who say that it would be a disaster if they achieved independence. Others say that they only want to live as individuals and do not care about anything else. I have met the whole spectrum, even those who say: "You are stupid to treat us so liberally. You force us to be more extremist because you allow the PLO to exist. Treat us as we are used to being treated." Others say that we are a paper tiger. I have never seen even a glimmer of justice in their demand for a state and have proved to them that this is the most counterfeit claim they could make.

In Judea and Samaria there are about eight hundred thousand Arabs. There is a similar number within the Green Line. There is an even bigger number in Transjordan. Why do those in Judea and Samaria deserve a state more than those in Transjordan? They are the majority in Transjordan anyway. But they did not want a Palestinian state there. In January 1965 they founded the PLO in East Jerusalem, together with King Hussein, in order to "liberate" Palestine. The Palestinian flag was to be raised only where the Jews had reached. Wherever the Jews were, that is where they wanted to establish a Palestinian state. The Arab states always used them. When these areas were ruled by King Hussein, he did not establish a Palestinian state for them.

The problem is that they want to replace us here. The whole of Judea and Samaria is six thousand square kilometers. Look on a map: on the one side is the Mediterranean, and on the other is Transjordan. Without Samaria, Israel is only fifteen kilometers from the coast to the border. Israel is one of the smallest countries in the world, even with Judea and Samaria, and it is a joke to establish a country, a so-called Palestinian state, on less than six thousand square kilometers.

Anyway, this is the heart of our country, the heart of our state. By rejecting partition, the Arabs did us a favor.

What are we looking for in the Land of Israel? Well, it all began here in Shechem [Nablus]. Here Abraham our father received the promise of the Land of Israel, as it is written, "And Abram passed through the land, to Shechem, to Eilon Moreh." Here the covenant with the Jewish people was established when they entered the land. Our right as Jews begins with that same promise, "To your seed I will give this land." After that promise we developed like all the other nations of the world. We were born here as a nation, we grew up here as a nation, and we were expelled from here and to here we have returned — it is that simple. Jerusalem, Hebron, and Shechem are the spinal cord of Judea and Samaria. How can anyone say to the Jewish people, "Okay, you will be a state without your spine"?

Assad and Umm Assad

The turning point in Palestinian history was the great disaster of 1948. During that year hundreds of thousands of Palestinian Arabs were turned into refugees, exiled from their homes. For over forty years they have languished in refugee camps, dreaming of awdah, or return. The generation exiled conceived of this return as a return to the towns and villages they remembered. Yet these towns and villages are no more; they have been destroyed, transformed, or buried. Their children, born in the squalid refugee camps of the West Bank and Gaza Strip and beyond, in Jordan, Syria, and Lebanon, are not prepared to wait any longer. They seek justice; they want a homeland and are prepared to pay the price, even if that means compromise with the Israelis or death.

We spoke with Assad and his mother, Umm Assad, in a refugee camp in the Gaza Strip.

Editors: How has the intifada clarified ideas of justice for you?

Umm Assad: We were very happy in our country, in our village, until the Jews came and slaughtered the Palestinians, like in Deir Yassin, where they killed the children on their mothers' laps, killed them until they fled. They cut open pregnant women and they miscarried; they raped women. We fled our homes because of what we had heard that the Jews did. We left everything behind and just came here, with nothing. We heard that whoever stayed behind would be slaughtered. We stopped for a short respite in Gaza City, and then we continued on until we reached this place, Rafah. We lived off what UNWRA provided for us, but life was very bitter. We suffered from all kinds of vermin, fleas, and lice in our clothes and on our bodies. It rained on us in the winter. We put up plastic bags, but the rain came down on our heads. When we arrived in Rafah, there were no houses for us. We received canvas and blankets. We lived in very bad conditions, but throughout those years we were told that we would return to our homes. They lied to us. Then there were arrests, and they killed us.

Then came the intifada, but that was started by the Jews. They killed four young men, cousins. They were returning from work, and a truck ran over them. Finally God raised us up and gave us rocks. Those rocks are from God. The intifada began with rocks. Wherever we could find them, we threw rocks at them. But they came and killed us.

At one o'clock in the morning they came into my house, and I asked what they wanted. They asked if there were any men here, and I said yes. I did not want to let them in, but they pushed me out of the way, went into the room where the boys were sleeping, and pulled them out of bed. They took the boys outside and forced them to clear the rocks. After they finished clearing the rocks, they were beaten and then returned home. This story repeated itself every day. They took one son who was studying at the university in Hebron. They said he was doing bad things. They demanded a 10,000-shekel fine. We gave them the money, but he was tried and imprisoned. Then they came again and took another son, who had been wounded. He was sleeping in his bed. Again they came in the middle of the night, not during the day. The boy wanted to go to university, to go abroad to study, and instead they came and took him. He is in prison for fifteen months. We are not well off, yet we paid their fines; life has to go on. But meanwhile they continue to arrest the youth, to kill them in the streets, killing women and using gas — you cannot imagine how many people have been injured by that gas. They torture us endlessly.

One side is armed, but the other is without arms. We have no arms — just the stones. There can be no justice unless they leave our country. Then justice would be done. Those Jews are enemies; they kill our children. What type of person can see a child shot dead before his eyes? If we had weapons, what would the soldiers do? Then they would bring in airplanes and bomb us out. The only justice is their leaving our country so that we can take care of our children, educate them and take care of ourselves. As long as they kill our men, there is no justice. Go visit the hospitals and see how many people have had their legs and hands broken, their eyes lost. When they go into the schools, they do not have mercy on the girls or the boys.

Eds.: When you say the Jews should leave the country, what country are you referring to?

Umm Assad: All of Palestine. We want all of Palestine and, most importantly, Jerusalem. We want to be able to pray there and visit there. We do not want these permits that keep tabs on our comings and goings. Jerusalem is our country, and God has created us there. When we were in our village, we lived off the land very happily. I go every year to visit the land of my village. How I long to return there, but the Jews destroyed it all — they even turned the cemetery into a forest. I cry over the soil when I see it. I take a bit of earth from there and cry over it as I return here. There is nothing better than the land that God gave us, and how I long to live on that land!

Eds.: Assad, what is your opinion of what your mother has said?

Assad: My mother left behind over two hundred dunams of land in B. My mother was exiled from her village, and we were brought here and had to live in a camp — the twelve of us in a four-room hovel. Everybody lives on hope; that is the basis of life. When my mother demands a greater Palestinian state, which includes B., Majdal [Migdal HaEmeq], Jaffa, and Isdud [Ashdod], it is because she lived on that land. She worked the land of B.; it is her right because she tasted of the sweetness of life there before 1948.

I was born here in 1962 in the city of Rafah. I was five years old when the Occupation began here. My earliest memories are of the soldiers following us in the orchards, firing their guns. When I asked what this meant, my mother told me about the Jews. Our parents reminded us of what had happened before, how the Jews had taken the land in 1948, how they had raped the women in Deir Yassin. On this basis my mother demands B., Majdal, Jaffa, and all of Palestine. We want the same thing, a democratic Palestinian state, including all religions — Jews, Christians, and Muslims — all living under the shadow of one state.

To return to your question concerning how the intifada has clarified the idea of justice, as you know, the intifada was not born on December 9, 1987, when it burst out here in the Gaza Strip. When my mother mentions the incident of the four young men killed then, that was only the straw that broke the camel's back. The intifada was born in the camps — in Jabalya, Khan Yunis, Shabura, and others — long before that. After a period it intensified. The intifada became better organized through the popular committees, which provided alternatives to the Occupation authorities. These committees helped the people, for example, during times of curfew. This alternative leadership dealt with problems without our having to refer to the Occupation courts.

In our war against the Jews we have used the most primal form of weapon: the stone. They use bullets and gas. Our aim in throwing the stones is not to kill the Jews, not even to wound them. We are not going to achieve a Palestinian state through this. When we attack a military position, it is because we are trying to defend our rights.

Our rights, which we are demanding now, include the establishment of a Palestinian state in the territories occupied in 1967 — the West Bank and the Gaza Strip. The PLO has suggested a number of peace initiatives, but Israel has refused them all. Does Israel think that a Palestinian state is a monster? A state that includes the West Bank and Gaza Strip is the least that can be done to recognize our rights. Look, they are bringing Jews from Russia and Romania and settling them here in the Occupied Territories. It is our right to have a state here and bring home our exiles from Lebanon, Jordan, and Syria. As you know, the Palestinian people today includes about five million refugees. The least one can do is allow them to live under their own flag with their own identity. We in Gaza are provided at the moment with Egyptian travel documents, which allow us to travel within the Arab world, but we are forbidden from travelling outside, to America or Japan. We are demanding a passport, an identity card, and a flag. We want a state that would have foreign embassies in every country, just like Israel at present.

Eds.: Umm Assad, what do you think of the youthful leadership of the intifada?

Umm Assad: Their identity is Palestinian, of that same Palestine, Jerusalem, and the land we were exiled from. They say: "We will die, if only Palestine lives. Palestine is our land." They say this in front of the soldiers.

Eds.: How has the intifada affected the relationship between the youth and their parents?

Assad: Some have pointed out that the ones leading the demonstrations were born after 1967 — that is, under the Occupation. We call them "Saturday's children" because their fathers worked in Israel and they had one day a week off, Saturday, when they came back to the Gaza Strip to be with their wives. These youth are nineteen or twenty years old now. They have grown up under the very difficult circumstances of the Occupation. They have witnessed their rights violated in the schools and in their homes and in every place. They have grown up in a world where everything has to pass through the civil administration and the secret police. They face difficulties and obstacles at every turn. This generation has internalized these problems. Many of these youth were wounded, which led their parents to an understanding of the situation. Then they too began to participate in the uprising, men and women together. How can parents watch their child being shot dead in front of them, or being beaten in front of them?

The intifada has influenced the relations between parents and children in my own house. My brother, twenty-two years old, was taken in March 1988. I was sleeping when the soldiers came in, waving their weapons in my face. "What's going on?" I asked. I was surprised at their being here at such an early hour — about one o'clock in the morning. They said, "Get dressed!" And then they stood us up against a wall. I thought that they had come to get me. But they had come for my younger brother who had never caused problems. When they checked our identity cards, they told the rest of us to go, and they kept him. I was extremely shocked that they took him. They locked him up for three months. The same thing happened with my brother, who was eighteen. Again it was about midnight when the army came. They arrested him and sentenced him to fifteen months in prison, accusing him of being involved in the popular committees.

I too was taken in, as I was returning one day from Jerusalem. In Gaza City some youths were detained by a special unit of the secret police, and I was taken with them. I was put in prison, although I had no idea why. I asked why I had been arrested but received no answer. I was kept in prison for forty-two days without being interrogated, without anyone asking me even one question. After the first eighteen days I was sure that I would be released but was taken by surprise when the judge extended the period of detention for another thirty days. I demanded to know the reason. The translator warned me that if I did not shut up, the extension would be open-ended, meaning that I would never get out. So I shut up. But you discover in the prisons that human life is worthless; it has no value whatsoever. We were awakened at five in the morning and had inspections outside in the rain. I wanted to ask for a lawyer, and I went to the soldier guarding us. The sun was beating down, and I was feeling sick. The guards were playing backgammon and told me to wait. I waited until I could not take it any more. As a result I was in solitary confinement for four days. The whole system of trials and military courts is absurd.

Eds.: Umm Assad, what are the chances of reaching a just solution with the Israelis?

Umm Assad: Please God, someone will come and bring us a solution to these problems! Israel is a liar and does not want a solution. How many years have we already been in exile? More than forty. Israel says it wants a solution, but in the meantime it continues to kill the people with gas, grenades, and bullets.

Assad: In my opinion Israel will never make peace. We have had a brutal experience of Israel. We have compromised greatly in the peace initiatives, but Israel relates to us as terrorists. The youth who throws a stone as he stands facing them with their Kalashnikovs, M16s, and other weapons is called the terrorist. Children four or five years old are termed terrorists. The only thing is for pressure to be exerted on Israel by the Security Council members. They should force it to accept the establishment of a Palestinian state in the West Bank and Gaza. Otherwise the Arab countries need to unite and change their regimes, exchange the corrupt ones of the present for real revolutionary and free regimes, which could then fight Israel. Israel understands nothing except force.

Haim, Vladi, Dimitri, Haya, and Ida

The intifada is the most recent confrontation between two national movements that lay claim to the same land. Although the forms of the confrontation change, the basic issues remain the same — the right to live on the land, own the land, rule the land. In the midst of the intifada a new wave of Jewish immigration to the land began. The Jews see this as an inalienable right; it is not simply immigration but aliyah (ascent), kibbutz galuyot (the ingathering of the exiles, homecoming). Yet the Palestinians see this immigration of foreign Jews as resulting in their own displacement from the land of their forebears. While Palestinian refugees dream of awdah (return to Palestine), Zionism promotes mass Jewish immigration. When Russian Jews arrived by the thousands, dozens of Palestinians were deported, and hundreds of Palestinian homes were destroyed.

We spoke with five Russian Jewish immigrants to Israel in an immigrant absorption center in Beer Sheba.

Editors: How long have you been here, and why did you come?

Haim: We have been here for two months; we came here straight from the Soviet Union. We had very little idea about what is going on here in Israel. Any information we got was very negative. In the Soviet Union, all the nationalities have their place. They have their republics and their culture. The Jews, though, have nothing there. They have no place to live, and they constantly feel oppressed. In the Soviet Union every group has the right to preserve its traditions — except the Jews. They have no chance of preserving their traditions, and they cannot do what they want. There is a growing sense of despondency, and we do not know what will happen to those Jews left there. At any time there could be a disaster.

Eds.: What type of oppression are you talking about?

Vladi: You know things are very tough now in the Soviet Union. There is a shortage of everything — soap, shampoo, other essential commodities. In this situation people want a scapegoat for the situation. This is why there is hostility to Jews. Because of the democratization process certain neo-Fascist organizations emerged that are very anti-Semitic. I did not feel the pressure myself, but it is well known that Jews cannot reach the same positions as other Russians. Jews have to work much harder to achieve the same results as Russians. Jews are not accepted at some universities and some institutes; they do not get equal jobs, especially jobs connected with security. This is not admitted openly, but it is an unwritten rule. Sometimes it is said openly, loudly, and clearly: Jews are not welcome here!

Dimitri: In the Soviet Union the organization PAMYAT has proclaimed that it will get rid of every Jew. These people have even said that they will check for Jewish grandfathers or grandmothers and that all Jews should be killed or exiled. We heard about this organization through the press and saw things about it on television. It is quite well known.

Eds.: How do you think your lives will be different here?

Haim: First, we feel that we are equal here. This is very important for us. We are free here. You can choose to do whatever you like. You can live wherever you want, work wherever you want, travel wherever you want. You can go abroad if you want, which is quite a problem in the Soviet Union. If you do not succeed here, at least it's not because of your nationality. It's up to you. We feel comfortable here. We are not afraid that somebody will call out to our children, "Jews!" The atmosphere here is secure. You can walk at night without being afraid. Discrimination in the Soviet Union is felt everywhere, even in kindergarten. Even little kids know who the Jews are, and they do not accept them. Their parents have already told them that to be Jewish is to be bad.

Vladi: It is difficult now to say anything for sure about our future here. We really do feel independence and freedom here. We feel we can work here and achieve something. In the Soviet Union we always suffered from a lack of money. We were worse off economically, and we were continuously in need of commodities. It was a problem just to survive. Relations between people there are very tough. People do not even smile at each other. If you walk along the street, you see people looking very serious. People have a lot of problems, but here it is different. Here we get real help, not only material but also moral support. Unknown people come to our homes and offer us assistance. This makes us very happy.

Dimitri: I decided to come to Israel because I am Jewish. I wanted to live in a free country. Here I am not afraid. In Russia I was afraid because I was Jewish and a little better off than most, with a small flat and a small cottage and a car. Here in Israel I am a free man.

Haya: Although we did not have enough information about Israel, we always felt that we should live here because of our nationality. We did not believe the information we received in the Soviet Union about Israel because we are a people who have learned not to believe anything. We felt that the situation here was different, and now we see with our own eyes that things are not tough here. In the Soviet Union they show Jews arriving in Israel at the airport. Every day there is a political program that shows these Jews being put onto buses and being taken to the Occupied Territories. The program says that they have no choice; they are put there, and there they will have to defend Israel. But most people there do not believe this, and it does not influence those who have already decided to leave the Soviet Union for Israel. We have a lot of friends here from the Soviet Union and many more there who are coming. We do want peace; we do not want to fight here. We only want to live our own lives, to be safe and happy and live in peace.

Ida: We are happy to be here and to work here. We hope to build something good here. We hope to make a contribution to this country. I have been here more than two years, and when I arrived here, I received what I expected, exactly what I wanted. I feel comfortable.

Eds.: What about the conflict with the Palestinians? What about the intifada?

Dimitri: In the Soviet Union we read that there is a conflict between the Israelis and the Palestinians. We were told that the intifada was a peaceful struggle, but here we see it is actually a partisan war. We believe that these Occupied Territories historically belong to Israel but that the Palestinians should stay there and share equal rights. We are for peaceful coexistence between Palestinians and Israelis. We do not want to give the territories to the Arabs; they should be ruled by Israel. But the Palestinians should stay here and enjoy all that Israelis have.

Ida: Israel is not recognized by the Palestinians. We say that all people should live in peace here, Israelis and Palestinians. We are against this partisan war. We are against terrorism. We want to live in peace and comfort, and we oppose all war. The Palestinians should accept Israel and should accept things as they are.

Haim: We are for peaceful resolution of the conflict. Each side should accept the rights of the other side. We are tired of fighting. We do not want to fight anymore. We were taught that all life was a fight, but we do not accept this anymore. We came here to live in peace, and we do not want to fear for the future of our children. Our children should not have to be afraid.

Ida: Both sides should stop fighting and start living. If they do not agree, then the resolution should be through peaceful means, political means.

Haim: We do not understand why people should be killed for the sake of these ideas. Blood should not be spilled for this.

Haya: Israelis understand the Palestinians. It is the Palestinians who do not want to live with Jews. They do not accept the Jews in the territories, and we oppose this. We want peaceful coexistence.

Haim: In wars like these, people forget what they are fighting for. We do not understand the fight and do not see its purpose.

Dimitri: Soviet Jews have many problems, and they do not have time to think about the Palestinians. There we had basic problems, like lack of food and work. Now in the Soviet Union there is a revolution. We know that revolution means Jewish blood, our blood. I think that the Israeli-Palestinian problem is not a regional problem but a world problem. In my opinion this problem will be decided by many different countries.

Haim: There should be mutual recognition. That is the only way to solve the problem. The first step is to stop all provocations, all terrorism. Two neighbors cannot coexist when one is trying to harm the other.

PART 2

ACTIVISTS

Rami Hasson

Faced with a civilian uprising, some Israeli soldiers sent into the Occupied Territories to crush the intifada found themselves in a severe moral dilemma. Trained to stand against armed enemy soldiers, they found themselves facing instead stone-throwing youths, distraught mothers, and an entire enraged people. These soldiers found themselves unable to carry out military orders, disgusted with an army that they had been proud to serve in the past. Yesh Gvul (There Is a Limit), a popular movement advocating limited conscientious objection founded during the 1982 Lebanese War, gained strength. Members of this group informed the military authorities that they were no longer willing to patrol the Occupied Territories and that if they were not posted to military bases within Israel during their reserve duty, they would refuse military service. Over 130 Israelis have been sentenced to periods of imprisonment in the Israeli military jails rather than serve in the Occupied Territories.

We spoke with Rami Hasson, a Yesh Gvul and anti-Occupation activist, who has served four periods of imprisonment for his refusal to serve in the Occupied Territories.

Editors: We would like to know how the intifada has helped to clarify the idea of justice within the Israeli-Palestinian struggle.

Rami: For me it did not clarify it that much. My decision to refuse to serve in certain areas of the Occupied Territories matured before the intifada. Even without the intifada I would have reached this decision; in fact, in October before the intifada broke out, in my last military reserve duty, I knew that I would not serve in these areas again. The rest of the public believed that everything was very good for the Arabs under the Occupation, that they had not had it so good in the Jordanian period. Many people were quite convinced of this.

The critical problem here is that there are two peoples on the same plot of land. Neither of them has any other place. The only way to justify one's fears is to say that the other has it easier. The Jews often say, "Look, they have twenty-two other states, and we do not have even one." There is a search for justification without even listening to the other side. I formulate and listen only to my own arguments, and this is very comfortable. It is much easier to do this when there is nobody shouting on the other side. But now there is a whole people standing there and saying, "We cannot take any more; we are not prepared to take anymore." Even the women and children are involved — not, as it was comfortably depicted years ago, only terrorists.

Today you will not hear the argument that they have it good. The intifada was an eye opener. Before, many people said that there was no way to establish two states here, that this is one country. But now no one crosses the Green Line into the Territories. For years they erased the Green Line. This was official policy. They never admitted it, but not one map now in any school still marks the Green Line. Pupils should know, at least historically, where it was. They simply erased it, but today in the area everyone knows exactly where the Green Line is. Even in united and greater Jerusalem, people simply do not cross over to the other side. There is an unmarked border in this city, and people know exactly where it is. As for the argument about the impossibility of establishing two states — well, in fact they already exist and thus are possible.

In addition, the argument that the Occupation has no effect on us, that we can live like this for years on end, has also been exploded. Moral corruption has already reached the highest levels. The fact that the Occupation corrupts is undeniable, and people are aware of it. All these things help the masses to understand better the concept of justice.

The justice, quite clearly, is two states for two peoples. It is indeed very just that the Jews should have the whole country. It is also just that the Palestinians should have the whole country. Each side has enough arguments to convince you if you do not hear the arguments of the other side. This is the basis of the problem — both sides are very justified. The only way that you can allow for both nations to live here is by having some kind of compromise. Each one has to say, "I am indeed justified, but I have to compromise to live here in peace."

It was very easy for the Jews to bring up their very tragic past. They could always use the image of David and Goliath and claim that the Muslim world, the Western world — in fact, the whole world — was against them. This has become more complex because it is hard to play David against the Palestinians. It was easy for the Jews to point out Palestinian violence. Today after two years of the intifada, relatively few Jews have been killed by Palestinians — not just coincidentally but intentionally, because the Palestinians decided to use only a certain level of violence. That violence is even too great for my taste, but it is exercised with a great amount of restraint.

So it is difficult now to depict the Palestinian as bloodthirsty, as many people do. Moreover (and it might not be too pleasant to mention this), Jews lived very well under Muslims throughout history. I myself am from the Oriental Jewish community; my family has been here since the expulsion of the Jews from Spain. I am the twenty-ninth generation in this land; we have been here some five hundred years. There was Christian anti-Semitism against the Jews through most of history, but as far as the Muslims were concerned, there was none. Jews lived among Muslims in the Arab lands and even in Europe; the Golden Age was under Muslim rule in Spain. Problems between Muslims and Jews exist primarily because of nationalist reasons, since the beginning of the Zionist movement. Most Israelis and most Jews have ignored this, but today it is more difficult to ignore because we are penetrating the roots of the conflict. Today one can see that the reason for the hatred is the war over this little piece of land.

Eds.: Do you feel that the solution of "two states for two peoples" is really justice?

Rami: It is a little difficult for me to accept, for I really do believe that one day there will be no states in the world. If I were not Jewish, though, I probably would feel more comfortable with a bi-national state. There are a number of problems with this. First, it has not proved itself in the rest of the world. It would seem that not until every nation and fragment of a nation has its freedom will the flag of nationalism be laid down.

I am not religious, but I think that the world has and should have a vested interest in conserving the Jewish people in the Land of Israel. It is like a living museum — the ancient language in the ancient places. From a cultural point of view, we need a Jewish state at this point. It is a world interest. Yet when I look around, there are Palestinians to whom I feel closer than to certain Jews elsewhere. The same natural scenery speaks to us, the same experiences, even if it is sometimes from opposite sides. I do not believe in two alienated states. Quite definitely I believe in some form of confederation, two states that live together in close contact. I also definitely believe that it is possible.

Eds.: What motivated you to refuse to serve in the Occupied Territories?

Rami: I was doing my last reserve duty in October before the intifada burst out. My whole unit was in the Jordan Valley, but I was sent as an individual to the Allenby Bridge. They needed a sapper to check those getting off the bus. There one could see the conqueror and the vanquished with all the ugliness of both sides. You could find there a wide spectrum of Israelis, including those who felt very bad in their role as conquerors and sometimes turned a blind eye even in cases of security, because they feel so uncomfortable with the work they have to do. Others really enjoy the power they have to humiliate others, even when there is no need to do so. On the Palestinian side one could observe the same thing: some are completely servile to the soldiers without any reason, trying to find favor; others are very proud, even in a provocative way, without any reason, although obviously both sides have good reasons for these behaviors. After all, the relations are of conqueror-vanquished. There you could see the Occupation at its ugliest, what the Occupation does to people and how it extracts those least pleasant qualities from inside them. When I was there, I realized that I could no longer help to perpetuate this. Afterward, when the intifada broke out and people were being killed, I could see no reason to carry arms there against an unarmed population. But this was not something that happened all at once. Thoughts about refusing to serve began in Lebanon, although I did not refuse there.

Eds.: How many times have you gone to prison for your refusal?

Rami: Four times, for five months altogether. I should say that my refusal is not refusal to serve in the Occupied Territories but rather refusal to carry arms against a civilian population. I realize that there is a degree of hypocrisy in my stand because if I serve in the Jordan Valley opposite Jordanian soldiers, I am still supporting the army that does these terrible things. I have drawn a line, though: I will not serve on bases from which soldiers are sent on missions against a civilian population. I do serve in the Occupied Territories opposite Jordanian soldiers, and I even serve on the Golan Heights, which is also occupied territory where the residents do not want us. I serve there for two reasons: a political solution with Syria does not seem likely in the near future; also because the population there is not Syrian but Druze and, more importantly, blood is not being spilt there daily. If the Druze would actively resist our occupation and blood would be spilt daily and if a solution with the Syrians seemed realistic, I would not serve there.

Each time I was in prison there was at least one other person who had also refused to served in the Occupied Territories. Since the beginning of the intifada a day has not passed without at least one conscientious objector being in prison. The number of conscientious objectors has now surpassed 130 since the beginning of the intifada. This number includes only those who refuse, were sentenced, and sat in prison. Yesh Gvul claims that the number of conscientious objectors is much greater. Many refuse but are not sentenced. They say the number is closer to one thousand.

I sat in prison with malingerers and other military offenders, mainly Oriental Jews. I really have a soft spot for what is referred to as "the Other Israel" — these less successful youth from slum areas and development towns. I have a background in working with these youths as a youth counsellor. These are the oppressed of our society. Their refusal to share in the obligations, like serving as good soldiers in the army, is justified because they do not get an equal piece of the cake. I have a lot of sympathy with them, and it is easy for me to get along with them. These people are not a barrier to peace, they do not speak of "the land of our forefathers"; the only ones who do so are a small group of Ashkenazis. The older generation of Ashkenazis, those who are settled on the established moshavim and kibbutzim, speak of the Territories as a part of our heritage. The masses of the people, including the Oriental Jews, might have a lot of fears about security, but they do not really want the Territories.

Eds.: This is interesting because the stereotype of the Oriental Jew is one who is very eager to serve in the army against the Arab enemy.

Rami: I do not agree with this stereotype of the Oriental Jew. The obsession with defense in the face of the enemy is expressed much more by the Ashkenazis. It is quite understandable in the light of the Holocaust. The need for a state in order to exist is much clearer. The Oriental Jews came here more out of religious-messianic motivations. They did not really escape from the Arab countries. Some of them lived very well there. There are few Jews who long for Europe. But there are many Oriental Jews who long for their countries of origin. It is common among Moroccan Jews to long for what they call "home" — Morocco.

The Sephardi community of Palestine, the pure Sephardis, have always been very moderate, possibly because they are veterans here. The veteran Sephardi community were aristocrats who served as a kind of mediator between the Ashkenazi establishment and the new Oriental immigration. For whatever reason, these Sephardi aristocrats are compromising by nature. From my father's house and my mother's house, I learned the value that all persons have the right to live in dignity, no matter what their age, status, salary, or dress. Most of these pure Sephardis feel uncomfortable with the present situation. Even their representation in the present Knesset — Yitzhaq Navon, for example — makes this clear. He was the person who suggested joint education and meetings between Jewish and Arab pupils.

Here is an example from my own home. Once a boy at school cursed my mother, and I fought with him. I returned home, bleeding a little, and my mother was startled and asked me what happened. I told her that somebody had insulted her and that I had fought him. She said, "Next time somebody curses your mother, bless his, and then the next time he will be too embarrassed to curse your mother." This is exactly the way we were brought up. There is something quite Christian in this. I do not know where they came up with this "turn the other cheek" attitude, but we were brought up on it.

When I was drafted, it was very difficult for me. I was basically a pacifist. War had begun in October 1973 and continued into 1974, and I was drafted at the beginning of 1975. I really hesitated whether I should declare myself a pacifist or not. It was quite a conflict because I knew that Israel really needs an army. Israel without an army will not exist. I knew then that I would be put in one of the four combat units. It was not easy in those years, and people were quite opposed to me. You could not turn down the prize units until you had been accepted, at the very last stage. But if you refused, then they would call you to an interview to question your reasons, and if they sounded political — which they always did — they would put it into their files. They make sure that you know that they see this as most unfavorable. I did turn down a training course for command positions, and because of this I faced a lot of problems. So you see, there was a background for what was to come later. My family and friends support me in all of this, and no one doubts my motivations, although many think I have gone the wrong way. Even among those who refuse, there are many discussions about what is the right way.

Another turning point was the visit of Sadat. I was a soldier then. I was watching television in the canteen, and they showed his plane landing. I was simply amazed. Until the door opened and they showed him descending the stairs, I was sure that this was some kind of trick. I even thought that maybe a whole platoon of Egyptian soldiers would pop out and shoot the entire Israeli political leadership that was gathered there. It was very difficult for me to believe. The monstrous image that they had tried to build in our heads of an Arab with whom you could never live in peace suddenly was depicted differently, and not only for me. After a short while Sadat was more popular among the masses here than Menachem Begin. This made me feel very optimistic about the masses. Suddenly we saw that the Arabs also wanted peace. Sadat was a very charismatic figure, and it was not difficult to believe him.

Eds.: But for Sadat there was no problem of refugees or of homeland but rather one of borders. The Palestinians demand a just peace. What do they mean by this?

Rami: Concerning the Israeli-Palestinian struggle, it is difficult for me to talk of a just peace. Justice for the Palestinians is the whole land without us. It's easy to see this as just, and it's easy to sound convincing on this point. I would not argue that a person who claims this is right or wrong. I might be able to accept partially some of the claims, but I would argue as to the realism of the solution and whether it is possible to live here in peace by ignoring the other side. It is easy, though, for me to understand the claims.

It is also easy for me to understand the claims of those Jews who claim that the world vomited them out, that they have no other place and that finally they are holding onto something here. They say they have no other place where they can live, and to my dismay this is repeated each time. This is repeated now concerning the flight from Russia, which is definitely not a Zionist immigration; it is flight from fear of extermination. Here too it is easy to convince me. It is easy to understand, even if it refers to a piece of land which that people owned two thousand years ago, even if at the expense of others. Justice is very difficult to carry out here. The problem is that there is one state here, containing two peoples, and it easy to understand the sense of belongingness of both peoples and their just claims. Is it possible to do justice here? It is impossible; only compromise is possible.

Eds.: You talk of Israel as a place to preserve Jewish culture, yet has the Jewish culture it preserves not been Ashkenazi culture? And has it not suppressed Sephardi and Oriental culture?

Rami: The pure Sephardis do not feel oppressed. Those who feel oppressed, and rightly so, are those Jews who came from the Arab countries, the Jews of the "redemptive immigrations," as they were called back then. These were the Jews who came whose culture was suppressed by Ashkenazi culture. Before this immigration the veteran Ashkenazi and veteran Sephardi communities each preserved its own culture. The Sephardis had been here since the Spanish expulsion. Then there were the "pioneer immigrations," the First and Second Aliyahs, the ones that determined the relations with the reality of Palestine. Until they came, there were excellent relations between both the Ashkenazi and Sephardi communities and the Arabs. These relations continued in most places even after these so-called pioneer immigrations. This continued until the two sides realized that they both had national ambitions for the same plot of land. Until that time relations were good, and the Jews were a point of curiosity for many Arabs.

Thereafter there was the period of the "rescue immigrations" from Europe, people who had fled from there because of anti-Semitic persecutions. When these mass immigrations from the Ashkenazi lands began, then the problem also began. When the mass immigrations began from the Arab countries, after the establishment of the state, they entered into an already-existing frame of relations.

Those who spoke Arabic stopped speaking it. Hebrew was a relatively new language for my parents, as I know from stories I heard from my grandmother. But there had always been a struggle to preserve Hebrew. They feared greatly that Hebrew would become extinct. The Sephardis here stopped speaking Ladino, a Judeo-Spanish dialect; they simply buried it. This was not intentional, but rather they were convinced that a new society was being built here and the language must be Hebrew. For me this is completely understandable. Likewise the Ashkenazi Jews simply stopped speaking Yiddish, a Judeo-German dialect, and transferred to Hebrew. So it is not a case of Yiddish dominating Ladino but rather the insistence on speaking Hebrew. My parents speak very good Arabic. Even the Ashkenazis of that period knew Arabic very well. Before the state, Arabic played a big part in the Hebrew slang.

The demonization of the Palestinians and the Arabs in general began after the establishment of the state. Borders were drawn, and this even worked on the older generation. They placed a barrier between people that did not exist before. This newly created hatred suddenly took on directions that are hard to understand. The generation of the Jewish pioneers characterized the Arab as a hero. The Arab was the big guy on the horse, a real hero, the exact opposite of the image of the Diaspora Jew. After the establishment of the state and the drawing up of borders, the hatred began. I have difficulty in finding its roots. I think hatred that should have been directed against Europe was directed toward the Arabs.

Eds.: Could you tell us how you see the connection between peace and justice?

Rami: Both sides are so overloaded with justice that if one of them insists on justice there will be no peace. There must be two states for two peoples. Each nation must be sovereign in the territory that will be decided as belonging to it. I am not necessarily talking about the Green Line. If they decide on any other border, it is fine with me, although I find it hard to imagine any other border that both sides might agree on. No one will be completely satisfied. Even if there are two states — the State of Israel within the Green Line, and Palestine in the territories over the Green Line — the two peoples will not be overly satisfied with the territories they receive. They will be satisfied that there is peace.

There are a lot of problems. Israel without the Territories is indeed small and problematic. The Territories existing as a state are also problematic. There is no exit to the sea, a state is cut in two, and passage is through Israel — there are 1,001 problems. Only a peace that can offer true security will distance people from their dreams of a Greater Israel or Greater Palestine. And this type of peace is possible. I really do see that the cooperation between Israel and Palestine will burst through the boundaries. It will help to topple the dictatorial or semi-dictatorial regimes around us. We can open an economic commonwealth of Israelis and Palestinians. It all sounds very utopian, but it is definitely possible. Possibly this idea can ignite the imagination more than ideas like "maybe I can return to Jaffa," or "Hebron should be mine."

Wafiq Abu Sido

The violation of basic human rights has been a feature of the Israeli Occupation since 1967. During the intifada the injustices of Occupation intensified as the Israeli Occupation authorities sought to crush the uprising. Methods to deal with the intifada included using live ammunition, rubber bullets, various types of tear gas, rampant beating, destruction and sealing of homes, imprisonment, administrative detention, deportation, tax raids, and land and property confiscation. Palestinian and Israeli organizations have worked tirelessly to document the full range of violations against human rights. Palestinian and Israeli lawyers have persisted in seeking justice beyond the spurious military courts.

We spoke with Wafiq Abu Sido, a resident of Gaza City and a human rights activist working in the Palestinian Human Rights Information Center.

Editors: How do you understand issues of justice in the Israeli-Palestinian conflict?

Wafiq: As far as the Palestinian people are concerned, there is no possibility for justice as long as there is Occupation, as long as there is another people ruling over them in the Occupied Territories. Zionists seem to believe that they are the best people in the whole world. Yet where is justice under this Occupation? We have lived with Occupation since 1948. We were uprooted from our land, our villages were destroyed, our cities were sacked. This was done under the slogan that the Jews were preferred by God and that they are the upper class of humanity. Over the past forty years the Israelis have proclaimed to the world that they are the ones suffering injustice, that they want peace but the Arabs do not.

The reality is quite different. They are the ones who do not want peace and are using force. We, as Palestinians, are searching for peace and justice. These two words go together, because there is no peace without justice, and no justice without peace. The world can see quite clearly the daily perpetrations of oppression under the Occupation — the killing of children, the beating and gassing of pregnant women, the destruction of houses. Where is the justice in the destruction of a house? If a child throws a stone or even a Molotov cocktail, why should the house of an entire family be destroyed and these people be forced onto the street? Where is the justice in a person being in the Israeli prisons, under torture for forty-five days, and then being released without any charges against him? They use all kinds of torture, including beatings and psychological duress. Is this what justice is all about?

We are active in trying to document human rights violations under the Geneva Convention and other international agreements. Israel talks about justice and peace, but it is not real. We do want peace. We want to live with them, but they exiled us from our land — Palestine. We want to live on our land. We recognize that they have become great in number; they have brought here the whole world, Jews from everywhere. But I want to live here too. I did not come from Romania, Russia, or the United States. I am rooted here, as was my father and grandfather. We both deserve justice. A just peace must be based upon my right to self-determination and the right of my family, now exiled, to come here and live with me. Just as the Israeli has the right to bring Jews here, so it should be my right to bring back Palestinians who are living in Jordan, Lebanon, Syria, America, Brazil, or Argentina. It is my right to have a state, just as the Israelis have a state and national existence. They have an army; I should have an army. If they want a demilitarized Palestinian state, then let them disband their army and get rid of the weapons they have.

Eds.: You are not from Gaza originally. What about returning to Jaffa, from where your family comes?

Wafiq: My family is from Jaffa, the city that before 1948 was known as the Bride of the Mediterranean. It is the right of all refugees from 1948 to return to the place that they left behind. But if the national leadership of our people reaches a solution to the problem that does not allow for this return, then we will stand with our leadership. We seek a solution and do not wish to destroy an Israeli kibbutz or moshav. We want to live in dignity, peace, and justice alongside the State of Israel.

Eds.: How did you become politically conscious and active in the field of human rights?

Wafiq: I was born in 1962 and thus was five years old when the Israelis entered the 1967 war. Bombs were falling right next to the house where my family was living. We moved the cupboard and storage boxes to support the roof just in case it collapsed on us. From that moment I remember that there was an Occupation, and I began to ask why it had come, why it was killing us. From the very beginning, at school we would read the newspapers and literature. We became especially conscious after the Beirut War. After 1982 we tried to acquire the necessary ideological basis for activity. We learned from the experience in Vietnam, from Algeria, from the Philippines, and we even read about Ben-Gurion and Menachem Begin. We learned from the experience of our families, and so we became capable of a struggle and a revolution. It takes time to develop this consciousness.

Eds.: Why is it important to document the violations of human rights?

Wafiq: First of all, Israel boasts that it is the only democratic country in the Middle East. It tells the world that the Israelis are the ones suffering injustice, that they just want peace, but the Arabs are criminals who want to kill all the Jews and throw them into the sea. For forty years they have been telling this story, but the Palestinians are conscious of this lie. We are now saying that we are, in fact, the ones who are suffering injustice; we are the ones living under Occupation, and we want to tell the world to come and take a look. Who really wants peace? We do not have all these nuclear weapons. All we want is some land upon which to live in dignity and peace.

The daily violations of human rights, whether by the authorities, the army, or the settlers, the arrests, killings, land confiscation, and so forth are crimes against our people. We must show the world, and especially the United States, which supports Israel so fully, that this is the Israel they are supporting. We must tell those Americans who care that they are standing alongside Israel, which does not honor the Geneva Convention or other international agreements, that Israel does not respect the human being as a human being but respects the Jews only. This is the reality of our daily lives. Why does the entire world and especially America justify these practices and not give us any support? During the intifada my own work has increased greatly. The Israelis have invented new methods of repression, and it is very difficult to keep track of the myriad of things that happen.

Eds.: Wafiq, what will you do after the establishment of a Palestinian state? Human rights documentation is relevant only under Occupation.

Wafiq: I will do the same thing. When there is an independent Palestinian state, we will have to continue our work in the field of human rights. Although the Palestinian people has lived through difficult circumstances, it cannot now start practicing human rights violations against other Palestinians. We now understand the value of human rights and the value of the human being. This is indeed present in our religious traditions, in the Qur'an and the Sunna, just as it is present in the New Testament and the Torah, and we must preserve these principles.

Dr. Veronica Cohen

The intifada stirred the conscience of many Israelis who found reports of Israeli brutality in the Occupied Territories deeply disturbing. In the first few months of the intifada, dozens of peace and protest groups sprang up, and demonstrations, vigils, petitions, and marches became a common feature of day-to-day life in many Israeli towns and cities. These groups organized activities to protest the violations of human rights, sponsoring solidarity visits to Palestinian homes, villages, and towns. Simultaneously they issued repeated calls for peace and dialogue with the Palestinians and their representatives. The marginal left wing, which had always called for a two-states solution to the conflict — Israel and Palestine side by side — found itself legitimized and within the popular consensus.

We spoke with Dr. Veronica Cohen, an Orthodox Jewish peace activist, one of the founders of a number of peace and protest groups, including Immigrants against Occupation, the Beita Committee, and numerous Jewish-Palestinian dialogue groups.

Editors: How do you think the intifada has helped clarify the issue of justice?

Veronica: My first reaction to this question is that it has not. How I behave toward the Palestinians has not changed during the intifada. For me what has changed is that before the intifada I had the feeling that this was an unjust situation of a dimension that was beyond me. It was like asking me what I feel about poverty. Do I think poverty is just? Is there anything I can do about it? I don't think so. I don't know where to touch it. There was a turning-point experience for me when I first really became active. At a meeting in my house somebody said: "I would like to do something that will succeed. You know that if people only wanted to, they could even end the Occupation." That moment something happened to me. It never occurred to me before that it could be done. But then something really turned in my head. Because of the intifada a lot of things have become possible in my mind. When I think of this question, I try to look at justice and peace. Are they in fact one term? Obviously not. We had peace before the intifada, for basically things were chugging along very nicely; if you did not worry about justice, then things were quite nice. There was cheap labor, a large market for Israeli products, and only minor amounts of terrorism. Things were pretty good. There was peace there. The issue, though, is reaching a just peace.

There is a story in the Talmud that I learned from my daughter, who brought it to our dinner table. It is a stark and disturbing tale that is crucial to the situation. You are adrift on a boat with several other people, hoping to be rescued. It will take a certain amount of time, and you alone happen to have a bottle of water, but just enough to keep you alive until you have a reasonable chance to be saved. Should you share your water with the others, knowing that if you do, all of you will die tomorrow? Or should you save yourself until help is available? The Talmud concludes that you should not share your water, because rationally you know that through this generous gesture you are actually choosing to die. But the end of the story is that a righteous man should share his water.

I think that this is the crux of the matter. For many Israelis, and for me too before the intifada, there was the feeling that if you behave in a just way toward the Palestinians, you are really endangering yourself. And that has changed for me during the intifada. How can I sit there and drink the water and watch everyone else die of exposure? In the same way, I could not stand to watch the Occupation, even though at that time I thought that by ending the Occupation, we were really endangering our whole existence. In that sense it has become easier to be just. I have less of a sense that by sharing my water I am certain to die. By getting to know Palestinians, the fear — which I think is really within most Israelis — has changed. I do not think it has disappeared, but it has changed in volume and in quality. I have talked to enough Palestinians so that I now no longer believe that a Palestinian state is necessarily a threat to our existence. I did not think this before, although to me that did not justify the Occupation.

We are not talking here about absolute justice; in fact, we are talking more about fairness than justice — a kind of equality of opportunities. If Jews deserve an independent country, then Palestinians deserve one too. Palestinians themselves say that at one point they wanted all of Palestine. Now they have realistically decided that although this one or that one owns a house in Yaffo [Jaffa] and longs to go back to it, this is not a possibility. But it is possible to have something and give up the right to something else. That is how they now see a just settlement, and that is also how I now see a practical, just settlement.

The man who longs for his house in Yaffo, however, is not going to give up longing for it because now they have a Palestinian state. That is why I am afraid that a two-state solution is just an interim solution. I am basically not for independent states. I think this desire is a negative element in human life, but as long as the world is divided up into nation-states and as long as Israelis live in a nation-state as the most secure arrangement for their survival, there should be equal chance. Therefore I think that the two-states solution is the necessary solution, although I do not think it is going to be the last. It is one step before the solution. It will lead to another war, I am sure. I do not think it will work. I wish we could jump to the solution that I think is the true solution: some kind of bi-national state. But I think no one is ready for that. I think it is very tragic that I am working for something I do not really believe in.

Eds.: Are you talking about a bi-national secular state?

Veronica: Yes.

Eds.: And as an Orthodox Jew, you can say this?

Veronica: Yes, I think that even as a religious person this will make things much easier. It will take away the necessity to be coercive about religion. To separate what is called church and state is good for the church and good for the state. That is my ideal solution, but I do not think anybody is really ready for it.

The two-states solution is not a workable solution because we are so intertwined, our lives so interwoven. The Palestinians who live in what is Israel proper are not going to want to move away from Israel because their life is already built here, and I do not know what is going to happen to the settlements, but very likely there are going to be Jews living in what is going to be Palestine proper. It's not going to work unless we have some kind of very friendly open-border policy or a confederation of some sort. I hope I am wrong. I think a two-states solution would be very nice. But I do not really foresee that is where it's going to stop.

Eds.: Did you grow up in a family that shared these concerns?

Veronica: I always remember myself somehow being obsessed with the freedom of the individual and fighting against oppression. I grew up in Communist Hungary in a family that opposed Communism. The turning-point experience may have been when I was about seven years old. I was born in the ghetto. I somehow miraculously survived. I remember hearing about the Holocaust day in and day out as people talked constantly about who did come back and who did not. Among my mother's best friends, I was the only one who had a father of all the children who I grew up with. Everyone else had perished during the Holocaust, including my uncle and my grandmother. My uncle was taken away by the Russians, and a major experience of my childhood was waiting in vain for him to come back.

When I was seven, we were taken to the circus. On the way there, I found out that this was not just any circus but a German circus. Now I had grown up and heard for seven years about "the Germans." As we got near, we saw a cluster of children gathered around some great attraction. I asked what it was. They answered that there was a little German girl. I could not imagine what a little German girl looked like but was sure she was a monster child, the Devil's daughter, standing out there. I was dying to see what this child looked like, but I was afraid to look at her. I suddenly looked at her, and — good Lord! — she looked just like me. And I remember that that really shattered me.

I went home and told my parents that I had seen a little German girl and that she looked just like me or anyone else, and I asked how that could be. And then I had long talks with my parents and found that my thinking really changed. I would talk with my father hour after hour, and he would teach me history as we walked to synagogue. He would explain to me again what happened after World War I and what the German suffering means, and he explained about why he thought it happened. I felt that I could become just as evil as what she represented, which made a big difference to me.

Eds.: Coming from this background, what are you now doing to promote this sense of need for freedom and justice?

Veronica: For me, meeting Palestinians is the most important thing. I really did once feel, like most Israelis, that they are a danger to our existence. Now I think this is largely an irrational fear, although in 1948 I think they would have very cheerfully wiped us out. If there is a cause for hope, then it is that people change, and I think that the Palestinians have changed. The whole world configuration has changed, but we are somehow stuck in our perception of 1948; we are in a kind of time warp. The world is changing, yet we are stuck there — thanks to our leaders, who are artificially freezing us in that perception.

When you start to meet Palestinians and you find out that their dearest wish is not to murder a Jew but to have a country of their own and to live as people with self-respect, that dissolves your fears. So I am trying to help other Israelis meet them. Talk is not enough. When you are afraid, someone telling you not to be afraid is not going to eliminate your fears. But when you go through experiences, then the fears, by themselves, begin to dissolve.

For example, for many of my friends to sleep overnight in a Palestinian village was an incredible experience. For many of them waking up in the middle of the night with their family in a Palestinian house was like their worst nightmare come true. There is not a Jew in sight, there are no soldiers and you do not have a telephone. Yet you say: "My Lord, it's all right, these people are actually my friends. Not only that, but if the soldiers come by, these Palestinians will protect me from them." This puts you in a very strange position of asking who my friends really are and who my enemies are. It forces you to define the world in terms other than "friends" and "enemies." You begin to dissolve those very categories — either that, or you go away. A lot of people left the peace movement because they could not deal with that issue of who my friend is and who my enemy is. The only way to get rid of this conflict though, is to get rid of those categories of friends and enemies. We must get to the level where we can say they are human beings. I think that when you go through these experiences, you begin to dissolve these categories. So that is why I try to promote dialogue. Dialogue is much more meaningful when it is there, in Palestine, then when it is here. It is the experience of being there, of being taken care of.

Another approach is to help Israelis feel a revulsion at what they are doing. So we take people to trials — military court sessions — and they suddenly come face to face with just how oppressive we are, with the full weight of the oppression. This might galvanize them into more action. People go home traumatized, I hope in a way that will make them more active.

I am trying to speed up the Israelis and slow down the Palestinians, so that they will not miss each other when the meeting time is supposed to come. I want to give Palestinians ways of dealing with their own suffering. On the micro-level, their daily lives are horrendous; on the macro-level, things are changing, and there is a hope for a solution. But they may give up before the solution comes. So what comes out of the meetings for them is things that make them more hopeful about Israelis. If they do not think that we are hopeless monsters, then maybe they will hang in there longer.

Eds.: Do you imagine that in your visits to Palestinian villages, the Palestinians perceive you in much the same way that you perceived that little German girl?

Veronica: For sure. It's a two-way street. I don't think that the Israelis are the only ones who need to learn. I think that in every dialogue group and in every meeting, both sides have a desperate need to learn. They are as ignorant of us as we are of them. They are as full of stereotypes and misconceptions as we are.

I want to tell you a story that I do not tell everybody because some Israelis would be frightened by it. Once I had a discussion with a sixteen-year-old Palestinian. We were at a military trial of some Palestinian youths in Nablus. We could not get in, and inside there was a Jewish teenager from Eilon Moreh. This Palestinian youth was looking at him and saying, "Look at him — he is so arrogant, he is so sure of himself, and he does not realize that all I want is what he already has." I thought, "What an intelligent child, and how reasonable," and I wished that Israeli children could be as intelligent and as reasonable. I said to him, "You know, I really agree with you. So how do you predict the future?" I was curious to see whether he was optimistic or pessimistic. But he misunderstood the question and he said, "Please do not be angry at me for saying this, but in the end we are going to kill you." I said, "Oh, really?" He said, "Yes, the Prophet Muhammad says that in the end we have to kill the Jews." Someone else in my group said, "Me too?" He replied, "No, no, not you," and for the first time he had to confront the fact that he talks about these absolute things but cannot apply them to a human being standing in front of him.

It's not that I think there are no Palestinians who would love to kill the Jews. I think that this boy was growing up with the notion that at some point it was his obligation to kill the Jews. I think it is not as pervasive as we think, and for now it is not the voice of the majority or of the leadership, and that is what is important.

Eds.: What is the force that drives you? You say that you are very realistic; you see all the dangers, the risks and the complexities. But what drives you to continue and not just give up?

Veronica: Everything is moving in the right direction but at the wrong tempo — the Israelis are moving toward the Palestinians and the Palestinians toward the Israelis, but we are going to miss each other. By the time the Israelis have changed, the Palestinians will have changed again toward using much more violence. There is the possibility of a historical moment, and I fear it is going to be missed. This is what drives me, trying to change the tempo of the Israeli change, because I think that it is changing, but it is not fast enough for what the Palestinians need. The sense of panic is that I can foresee this collision, and somehow I am trying to avoid it.

Faisal Husseini

Palestinian political leadership has finally received international recognition as a result of the intifada. It is now generally recognized that the Palestine Liberation Organization will be party to any resolution of the Israeli-Palestinian conflict. In November 1988, in Tunis, this leadership clearly pointed the way to direct negotiations with the Israelis on the basis of a two-states solution, Palestine and Israel side by side. Within the Occupied Territories those associated with the Palestinian national leadership, formerly continuously harassed and detained by the Israeli authorities, were sought out as possible partners for negotiation.

We spoke with Faisal Husseini, director of the Arab Studies Society (closed by the Israeli authorities for over two years now) and a leading spokesman for the Palestinian position in the West Bank and Gaza Strip. Despite his leading role in seeking a just solution to the conflict and his extensive talks with Israelis from the entire political spectrum, Faisal has been administratively detained for long periods by the Israeli authorities a number of times since the outbreak of the intifada.

Editors: Faisal, could you speak to the idea of the intifada's having clarified some of the issues of justice?

Faisal: I believe that the whole fight has been for justice. During the first year the fight was not only against the Occupation. It was not only a struggle between the Israelis and the Palestinians, but there was also a kind of internal fight within each Palestinian. This was a struggle between pure justice and possible justice, a struggle between the legitimate dream and the reality. This was a fight to find a new way to implement our aspirations, and at the same time take into account the reality of the situation. So if we start to talk about justice, we are not talking about pure justice but rather about possible justice within a reality that has been forced upon the Palestinian people. The result of this whole internal struggle was the resolutions of the Palestine National Congress on November 15, 1988, when we accepted the idea of a solution of two states. This was an acceptance of a Palestinian peace initiative.

The second part of the intifada's clarification of justice is that you cannot reach justice until you have obtained equality. An obstacle to equality is fear. One of the achievements of the intifada has been that it allows the Palestinian to get rid of this fear and to face the other side as equals — even if they have guns, even if they are firing at me, yet I can face them; even if they put me in their prisons, yet I will face them. This attitude reduces fear, and this is what the intifada has done: it has brought courage to the Palestinian people. The second step, after realizing that I am not afraid now, is that I have no fears of the future. This is what has enabled us to accept the existence of two states, a Palestinian state and an Israeli state. This step is facilitated both by accepting the principle of possible justice instead of aspiring to pure justice and by ridding oneself of fear. It is an amazing thing that the Palestinians have less power than the Israelis, but we have more power within ourselves than the Israelis. Therefore we are ready to accept the idea of having two states for two peoples, to enter direct negotiations, while they are still afraid of this.

Within the Palestinian community the intifada has also achieved a lot. One of the things that the Israelis have used against us is collective punishment. This has put all the Palestinians under the same fate. This equality has led people to address the issue of justice together. It is no longer acceptable that someone, because of his political, financial, or family position, can have a greater say over the decision making than another person. We are all under the same effects of this collective punishment, so no one can say, "I am superior to another." This fact, in itself, can lead to justice. We can find this in an exemplary way in the prisons, where we are all equal. For example, if I have ten cigarettes and another prisoner has only one, the conclusion will be reached that all the cigarettes should be distributed equally. This is something that the Occupation has challenged us with, and our response has been to search for more justice within our own society.

Eds.: You make a distinction between absolute justice and possible justice. Absolute justice is based on reason, upon logical and historical analysis of a situation, but how do you promote an awareness of possible justice?

Faisal: You must analyze reality to understand this. In our struggle with the Israelis we have had to realize that to reach real peace and security in the area, the two peoples must get rid of two things: their beautiful and grand dreams, and their nightmares. We have decided to get rid of some of our grand dreams. Instead of having our state in all our homeland, a homeland we inherited from our fathers and grandfathers, we are realistic in looking at history and deciding to accept a state in only part of our homeland, alongside the State of Israel.

Second, we must get rid of the nightmare. We cannot go on living in fear of the other side, that there will be another Deir Yassin or another Kafr Qasim, that there will be another destruction of three villages on the road to Jerusalem, that the Palestinians will again be driven from their villages to the refugee camps in the West Bank and Gaza, and then driven again from the West Bank to the East Bank to Lebanon, and then driven from South Lebanon to Sabra and Shatila, and then killed in Sabra and Shatila and also at Tel Zaatar. All of this is a nightmare for each one of us. I am wounded. This nightmare means that wherever I go, I am wanted like a criminal and that therefore I must make myself strong so that I am feared. Because I am strong, I will never accept any idea of peace before you implement everything that I demand. Therefore we must get rid of our grand dreams and these nightmares. I think we have succeeded, and I think that this success is due to our internal self-confidence.

When I speak of possible justice, I am referring to what can be done also from the perspective of the international community, not through force but through the moral perspective. There are a lot of things that one can do and implement, but from a moral point of view they will not be acceptable. This is sometimes true even of things that are legitimate but cannot morally be accepted. Sometimes when something wrong has happened, you cannot help but deal with it in a different way. An example is an illegitimate child. I cannot relate to him his whole life as an illegitimate child. But this is certainly part of his life and history. But I cannot deal with him throughout his life as illegitimate, and he cannot act as an illegitimate person throughout his life. If I exclude persons from the law, then I am giving them the opportunity to act outside the law. To put them within the law means that the law relates to them, and then the conditions can be set. Possible justice is not to punish them for having originated outside the law, although possibly from the perspective of pure justice you could do that. Such treatment would change nothing in the future, and the circle of problems would remain. So the situation here is one of illegitimacy in the past, but we have to see what we can do. From our point of view, this is how we see Israel. It is outside the law, and it needs legitimacy. It is to our benefit to bestow upon it legitimacy.

Eds.: Was there some turning point, some particular experience, that made you realize that you should do this?

Faisal: Before 1967 everything was pretty ordinary for me, but in that year everything changed. Before the war I was living in Cairo and as a Palestinian was searching for a way to return to Palestine. I was searching for any way possible to unite the Palestinians, the Arab world, the Islamic world, so that I would have a force with me to allow me to return to my land.

I started political life when I was thirteen or fourteen. In those years I joined the Muslim Brothers. Then I joined the Arab National Movement. Then I became one of the followers of Nasser. All through this, as I was moving from one place to another, I was wanted by one regime or another. And so I faced a lot of problems, in Egypt and then in Iraq and Syria, later in Lebanon and Jordan. In each place I had problems because I focused on the problem of Palestine, whereas each regime was concentrating on its own interests. I found myself as a Palestinian, wanted and unwanted. They wanted to put me in prison, they did not want me to exist. I remember the times when I was the last one to leave the airport, the last one to have my identity documents returned to me in a bus or a taxi. I would have the feeling that forty or fifty people would be waiting in the bus for two hours just for me. Then I would have to explain to them that I am from Jerusalem, a Palestinian, not a drug dealer or a criminal. I would sit and reflect on my situation and think of the one responsible for all this — that is, my enemy. I perceived the Israelis as a military machine, and this was my enemy.

In 1967 I entered Jerusalem and began to walk around the city. Suddenly I had to face a lot of things. Some of these experiences were painful, but others opened new windows for me to look out of. At the same time as seeing afresh what the Israelis were doing to us, I also began to distinguish between the authorities and the army on the one hand, and the people on the other. I would walk in Jerusalem and see them — old people, children, strong people, weak people, intelligent people, foolish people — all kinds, just like my own people. I saw an old lady carrying her heavy parcels, returning from the market, and I could see in her one of my own relatives who lost her sons and has no one to help her. She too is forced to go to the market and buy her provisions with no one to help her. So I began to speak more and more to the Israelis, hearing their stories of their suffering outside Israel, which I had not been ready to accept before. They too had been wanted and unwanted, just like me. So I began to understand that there is more to this whole thing then just them wanting to do evil to me. This was the beginning of my thoughts about pure and possible justice. Injustice had been done to me, and I wanted to lift it from myself. But how could I do this without transferring this injustice to someone else? We might forget that we are not the only people who have suffered. We might begin to think that we have more rights than others.

David Hammo

Over 55 percent of the Israeli population is composed of Oriental Jews, Jews from Asia and Africa who lived for centuries under Islamic rule. Although Oriental Jews are a majority, Israeli political leadership reflects the European Jewish elite. The Oriental Jews form a disproportionate part of the Israeli proletariat and have often been relegated to the periphery of Israeli life. Oriental Jews have been stereotyped as right wing, largely because they voted the Likud party into power in the 1977 elections. Oriental Jewish intellectuals (and recently also some rabbis) have opposed this stereotype. Numerous Oriental Jewish peace movements have been established, often focusing on the combination of socio-economic protest with a clear call for peace with the Arab world at large and the Palestinians in particular. Integrated for centuries in the Middle East, these Jews constitute an important bridge between Israel and the Arab world.

Ghassan Rubeiz spoke with David Hammo, an Oriental Jew and longtime peace activist.

David: I was born in 1938 in a small village near Fez in Morocco, North Africa. Our family had ten children, and we lived quite comfortably. My father was a merchant. In 1950 my father had to liquidate his business because of his Zionist activities, and we immigrated to Israel. The ambition of my father to live in a Jewish country was passionate but was of a religious-messianic nature. It was an ancient desire within the Moroccan Jewish community. I can only speak for the Moroccan Jews; I cannot speak for the Polish Jews, because I think that the Jews of Europe have a different history than Oriental Jews, living in Muslim or Arab countries.

When my parents first arrived in Israel, they went from being middle class to being impoverished. My father could not find work because he was about sixty years old. A very prominent businessman proposed that he serve as a doorman. As a young man, I thought that these problems would solve themselves within ten years. We believed in a gradual Zionism that would bring together all the Jewish refugees from the different parts of the world and would give rise to an exemplary society for all. I would not say that this dream has disappeared, but it has certainly remained a dream. What happened to the Jewish population of the Middle East and North Africa in Israel was not just on the socio-economic level; in addition, their culture was degraded. The establishment tried to wipe out the culture our ancestors had preserved for thousands of years.

In 1959 I completed my military service and then wanted to study architecture. At the same time I had to work to support my parents. I sought an opportunity to study architecture at night school but was told that there was no night school for architectural studies. Not all young people can study during the day, however, for some of them must feed their families. I realized then that university education in Israel is available only to a certain class.

As I could not study, I went to work as a construction laborer. After two years, I opened a small blacksmith workshop. Two years later, in 1963, I married a woman of Ashkenazi background, from Germany. This created quite a stir in the town where I lived. How could a Jew of North African origin marry an Ashkenazi woman? We did not care because we were young. I continued to develop my small business, which allowed me a relatively comfortable life and a certain independence of spirit. I was not blinded by the Israeli system. In 1964 my son was born. In 1967 there was the war. I served in the armored corps in the Golan Heights. It was there I realized that the Israeli myth about the Arab soldiers who always ran away was only a myth. I saw them fight.

If there was a turning point in my becoming wary of Zionism, it was that war. For the first time I understood that this system would arrive at a dead end. I realized the humiliation of those three hundred million Arabs who were defeated by Israel, and I identified with their humiliation. It was the humiliation of my father because he came from the Arab world. During the 1973 war I understood the motive of the Egyptians and the Syrians, which was to wipe out the humiliation of 1967. I tried to explain this to other soldiers, but I was called to the tent of the lieutenant general and accused of demoralizing the troops. I think that in 1967 Israel was afraid of being exterminated. I am not sure that this fear was based on military or political reality.

It was certainly based on the history of Eastern European Jews. Their anguish and fear of extermination have been magnified by the Holocaust. The Ashkenazi Jews dominated the majority of the population, which consists of Oriental Jews, whom they had succeeded in polarizing. These Ashkenazi Jews felt masters of the world. But 1956 had seen the turning point of Israel toward imperialism. Until 1956 Israel did not identify with the forces of imperialism and reaction in the world. In 1956 there was a pact with the Western world against the Eastern bloc. This increased because the Ashkenazi Jews identified with Europe, even though the Jews of Eastern Europe had never really qualified as Europeans. They had been persecuted and downtrodden. In 1967 the Israelis presented themselves as supermen who make order in the Middle East.

I am part of a social movement in Israel that is very profound, and I believe that this movement is going to influence the future of Israel more than Zionism did. We realized that the mass of Oriental Jews would not be mentioned in Israeli history because they do not write that history. Israeli historiography had been the preserve of Ashkenazi Jews. It would be written that Israel had been founded by Jews coming from Eastern Europe, who had created the national

Zionist movement. There would be no mention of me or my footsteps. Once I had realized this, I decided to study at the university to gain knowledge about my society. My ideas were already formed by then, as I was thirty-seven years old. After three months I realized that I was studying in an Ashkenazi university for Ashkenazi Jews. I studied sociology and anthropology, and American-derived theories were used to explain the relations between Ashkenazis and Oriental Jews. One day I said to the teacher, "This is not relevant to the reality that we are living." He said that he thought I had slipped into Marxism. I said that I did not care whether this was Marxism or Maoism — all I wanted was something relevant to the society in which I lived. And so we founded the movement Yated, which aimed at a cultural revolution, a cultural renaissance of Arab Jews in Israel.

Later we realized that the problem was not a cultural one. The Ashkenazi system has created an ethnic and national hierarchy, and we, the Oriental Jews, were only a little higher than the Palestinian Arabs. The system is capitalist, sustained by America and the American Jews. It is necessary to overthrow this structure to change our country. We began research in the development towns, interviewing people. At first these people repeated hackneyed slogans, telling me that in the State of Israel "all Jews are brothers." When they opened up, however, they began to say that they were in exile in their own country. We began to establish little groups of activists that, in the beginning, focused on social problems in Israel. Later, people began to realize that the Israeli-Palestinian problem is at the center of the whole structure of Israel and is what prevents Israel's integration into the Middle East. We Oriental Jews were the ones who wanted open borders with the Arab countries.

These ideas spread, and new groups were formed, like TAMI, which is Oriental Jewish and semi-Zionist. There was a revolution on the television, which until then had denied our existence. I said on television that what was needed was an Oriental Jewish revolution that would make a pact with the Palestinians. I said that the establishment of a Palestinian state was in fact in the interest of Israel. What I said did not go down badly in the development towns. The following day I was not stoned. The population of the development towns turned to me and said, "David, when it comes to the social problems, we are with you, but you should be more moderate regarding the Palestinians." But they did not reject me. This is the same population that votes for Yitzhaq Shamir and Ariel Sharon. The future of Israel lies with the Orientals, and it depends on the development of an Israeli-Arab-Hebrew culture.

The concept of the Arab world wanting to exterminate Israel is just a myth upon which Zionism has based its effort at unifying Jews, despite the class struggle inside Israel. When socio-economic protest begins, the government says: "Listen, you are shaking the boat, and we will all be drowned. The Arabs are waiting to swallow us up." That is how the government has eliminated or co-opted these protest movements. But that does not work any more. The whole system is breaking down. SHAS, an Oriental Jewish religious movement, received six seats in the last Knesset election. People said after these elections: "We are reverting to the Middle Ages. SHAS will make the Oriental Jewish masses religious fanatics." But in fact SHAS has given a kind of legitimacy to non-Zionism in Israel. SHAS is not Zionist.

We need to organize in order to establish an alternate education system because the Israeli education system prepares 80–90 percent of Oriental Jewish pupils for blue-collar jobs. They do this with the Israeli Palestinians too. That is why we preach a covenant based on common interests, one between the workers in the development towns and the Palestinians. People have problems with this idea because it is quite new. There are fifty thousand unemployed in the underdeveloped development towns. One does not even know the statistics for the Arabs, but maybe the numbers are lower because they are prepared to work for lower salaries.

Editor: How do you see the intifada?

David: The intifada has increased fear of extermination. I should not call it fear but rather an extermination complex that exists almost as an official ideology of the State of Israel. This complex reads, "You see the Arabs now; they will begin with a Palestinian state, and afterward they will demand all of Israel." Yet, there is another, growing tendency to sympathize with the Palestinians, who face the strongest army in the Middle East. This second tendency leads to a demolition of the myth of the fearsome Arab and to a simultaneous humanization process. These two tendencies, fear and sympathy, have become confused. A young man from a development town says: "Yes, I do admire them. They persist, and they are ready to die; they are ready to do anything!" Two months later he has to go to military reserve duty, and then he says: "They want to exterminate us.

They are not talking about Nablus, Jericho, or Jenin but about Jaffa and Haifa."

The Ashkenazi elite wants a resolution based on separation. During the elections the Labour Alignment spoke of putting up some kind of electric fence between us and them like the one between Israel and Lebanon. Yet this Ashkenazi elite sees that any solution threatens its status in Israeli society, and therefore they want to try to perpetuate the system as it was before the Occupation. Those Oriental Jews who vote for the Likud hear Shamir, who says: "Listen! Intifada or no intifada, the Arabs are the same Arabs, the Jews the same Jews, and the sea is the same sea." That is to say, They simply want to throw us into the sea. But I would say that this population votes for Shamir not because of his ideology of force but rather because he represents an opposition to the Labour party, which is responsible for the class system. A vote for the Likud is not really for the Likud but against the Labour party, which represents the Ashkenazi hierarchical system. The world needs to know this.

Eventually there will be a Palestinian state, and this has penetrated the dreams of every Israeli. Everyone knows that it is inevitable, just a question of time. The Palestinians only need to continue what they have been doing for the past two years. I heard what the Fatah committee decided in Tunis, and that was a wise move. They have forced us into a corner where we have to make peace with them. They now say what we need to hear: "We do not want war; we want to live with you." And Israel is lost for words.

The decisions, though, are no longer being made in Tunis but in the Occupied Territories. It is a pity that the final decision will be made by the U.S. State Department and in Moscow. It is a pity because I think that Israelis could still stretch out their hands to the Palestinians and together they could work to correct this warped social system.

We must talk about future economic relations. If the Palestinian bourgeoisie thinks that it will continue its comfortable life in its beautiful villas and send us two hundred thousand unemployed Palestinian workers, they are mistaken. This would not be peace, and we must regulate the economic arrangements now, before it is to late. Otherwise we will have Israel as a First World country and Palestine as a Third World country. I have a great fear that the Palestinian bourgeoisie will collaborate with the Ashkenazi elite and leave the great mass of both peoples exploited. We need to begin to fight against that eventuality together.

Oussama Halaby

Among the Israeli soldiers patrolling the Occupied Territories are members of the Druze community, invaluable to the army because of their fluency in Arabic. Stereotyped by Palestinians as particularly brutal, they have been accused of perpetrating some of the worst cruelties. Being Palestinian Arabs, Israeli citizens, and members of the Druze religion, they have found themselves at the center of the Palestinian-Israeli conflict. Unlike their Muslim and Christian Arab compatriots within Israel, the Druze have been called up to serve in the Israeli army. The Israeli establishment prides itself on its relations with the Druze, using them as a showpiece of non-Jewish integration into the Jewish state. For decades the Druze religious leadership have cooperated in enhancing this image. The intifada has had far-reaching consequences on the community and its future orientation.

We spoke with Oussama Halaby, a lawyer active in human rights work in the West Bank and author of a study on Israeli policy toward the Druze.

Editors: You are a Palestinian Arab from inside Israel, a lawyer working on issues of human rights in the Occupied Territories, and a member of the Druze community. How do you combine all of these roles?

Oussama: It is not difficult to explain all of this and how it connects with the theme of justice, which is the topic of our discussion. Being a member of a minority in Israel is my starting point. Justice for me includes the value of equality. The authorities in Israel constantly speak of giving equal rights to all people in Israel, including the members of the "minorities." At the same time, they argue that only those who fulfil their full civic obligations in Israel will, in fact, be granted their full rights and full equality. It is here that we come to the Druze. This part of the Arab national minority in Israel can illustrate the whole problematic situation that we face. The Druze serve in the Israeli army and, according to the Israeli understanding, since 1956 have been fulfilling their full civic obligations and duties. Yet they have not been granted full rights. This fact raises questions about the intentions of the Israeli authorities.

After having completed some research about this problem of the Druze, I am convinced that the Israelis never intended to give full rights to anybody who is not Jewish. This state was established as a Jewish state. One of the High Court judges, Dov Levin, said in a judgment concerning the Progressive List for Peace, a leftist political party, that any political group that calls for full equality in Israel will be disqualified from running for the Knesset because a law states that every political group running for the Knesset has to accept that this state is a state for the Jewish people. I see no difference between the statement that "Israel is a state for the Jewish people" and that "Israel is a Jewish state." If a political group wants to run for the Knesset, it has to accept the fact that this state is a state of the Jewish people. I did not need the intifada to sharpen my understanding of the basic injustices present in the society here. I already knew this because of my being an Israeli Arab citizen.

For the Druze, the intifada certainly has influenced the community. I have met a lot of people from my community who have done military service in the Occupied Territories, and they have begun to ask a lot of questions. On television recently a Druze man of about forty was interviewed. He said that he had given many years of his life to service in the Israeli army, most of this period spent in the West Bank. Later, after he had been injured, he was not offered any assistance or compensation by the authorities. He said that today, if his son were to refuse to serve in the Occupied Territories, he would not interfere in this decision.

Eds.: How has the intifada clarified the issue of justice in the Israeli-Palestinian conflict?

Oussama: I think that occupation runs contrary to justice. Occupation means ruling another people, another territory by force. An occupier cannot rule according to the values of equality and justice. If the intifada has helped me at all, it is to make some of these points clearer.

The intifada shows that the entire military court system is an unjust one. The prosecutors and the judges are connected administratively with the same office — the military advocate general of the Israeli army. Soldiers arrest a youth who is brought to court. The prosecutor asks for a quick trial, the judge complies, and a pseudo-hearing follows. The first arrests, the second prosecutes, and the third passes sentence — yet they all belong to the same branch. This is certainly not justice.

Another point concerns house demolitions. Demolishing the house of a family because one of its members commits an offense far from home is unjust. You are either punishing an innocent family because of someone else's offense, or you are punishing the offender twice for the same offense. These two things contradict basic principles of the Israeli criminal law as I understand it. Let me give you an example. I represented a mother and her sons from Ramallah some time ago in a petition to the High Court of Justice. This family's house was demolished because the man of the family had tried to force an Israeli bus off the road. To no avail I cited a case inside Israel in which a Jew brutally murdered a Jewish child. This murderer was sentenced to life in prison, but his house was not demolished. Yet this man committed the offense far from his home, and his family had no idea what he had done or even that he was planning to do anything. I even presented a medical certificate to show that this particular offender had definite mental and psychological problems, but the petition was rejected. Such inconsistencies are opposed to justice.

I have also written a study on land alienation in the West Bank that illustrates further the contradiction between occupation and justice. I have been aware of these issues for a long time, but coming to the Occupied Territories to work made it very real for me. This is on the level of human rights, but it is not difficult to translate this into political terms. The Palestinian people have the right to national self-determination. Denying them this right is contrary to justice. Is it right, after you have attained a state with the support of the whole world, to deny the rights of others in retaining what you have?

First, there should be no Occupation. It is time to be realistic, and the PLO has understood this. Peace in the Middle East primarily requires the establishment of a Palestinian state alongside Israel. Without accepting the Palestinian's right of self-determination, there is no way to reach peace in the area.

Inside Israel, where there is a big national minority, the key is equality. If the Israeli authorities want to reach the goal of equality, they can begin with reforms that are not too close to the "Jewish values" of the state. Certain laws have no connection with the Jewish character of the state and yet are discriminatory. For example, there is a legal order concerning travel tax that must be paid by those leaving the country. Paragraphs there talk about a "returning resident" and a "returning citizen." There are many differences in the privileges granted the two categories. Six conditions define the "returning citizens," one of them being that if they were not citizens, then the Law of Return would apply to them. This, by definition, excludes the Arab citizens, who cannot be considered "returning citizens." This means that if a Jew and an Arab travel on the very same plane, on their return the Jew alone will be recognized as a "returning citizen," which is translated into thousands of dollars of economic privileges.

Likewise, the authorities can grant equal status and budgetary allocation to the local councils and municipalities, and they can stop making the connection between military service and equal rights. This last issue gives the Israelis a good excuse for discriminating covertly against the Arabs. For example, the authorities, who know the Arabs do not serve in the military, say that they want only those who have served in the army for certain jobs, or they reserve certain residential areas for those who have done military service. A more blatant example involves a group of Druze who completed their military service and asked to live in a deserted Jewish settlement in Galilee. They were refused permission because they were not Jews. Such discrimination could be minimized, and the state could still remain Jewish.

Eds.: What has made you aware of these things, when most of your community — the Druze — are not aware?

Oussama: Well, I am part of a minority within a minority within a minority. I do not remember when I first began to think about what it means to be a Druze. I am from Daliyat al-Karmil, a predominantly Druze village near Haifa. In my village there is a small Islamic minority. They came from a village called Im al-Zinnat, which was destroyed in 1948. They settled in the peripheral areas of my village, so that now there are both Druze and Muslims there. They went to the same school that we did, and I never noticed any difference that really mattered. It was the first time that I came into contact with a different group of people, but the differences were not important. I went to school later in Haifa, to the Arab Orthodox College. There for the first time, as a sixteen-year-old, I was asked what it meant to be a Druze. Until that time I had never thought about this because my village was the world. The Israelis have tried to encourage an Israeli Druze consciousness among us. They have tried to say that the Druze here have only two identities — their Druze identity and their Israeli identity. They supposedly have no other affiliation, certainly not to the Arab nation. Druze children are taught that they are not Arabs because being an Arab is something negative. The authorities, in talking about the Druze as a separate group with a separate heritage, have turned them almost into a nation of their own. Although this attempt at fragmentation is clearest with the Druze, they have tried it with the whole Arab minority. They talk of "minorities," in the plural. This is an injustice in itself, for we are being used in a game to divide up the Arab national minority.

In Haifa I found myself explaining, to the people who asked, what the Druze are not. These people knew that the Druze go to the army, that the Druze are collaborators, and so forth. I had to think clearly how to explain to these other Arabs that I was one of them. It was clear to me before I came to the college that I was an Arab, but now I really had to explain this to them. They had heard that the Jews and Druze always went together. Since the state is not seen as positive, the Druze were also seen to be on the other side.

The years I spent in the college were the beginning of deeper thinking about the world, about people, and about the things I have to deal with in my life. After one or two years at the college, I felt completely integrated there, and I was completely accepted. At the college it was very easy for me to define myself clearly as an Arab, a member of the Arab minority in Israel. I was born a Druze, but I could have just as easily been born a Christian or a Muslim. The fact is that I am a Palestinian, a member of the national minority in Israel, and an Israeli citizen. These things can go together, although they raise a lot of problems.

One such problem is how the Druze, or any other member of the national Arab minority in Israel, can serve in the army that is occupying their people's land? The Druze are used as soldiers in the Occupied Territories, and the Israelis propagate the myth of their ferocity and cruelty as they did in the beginning of the intifada. Now it has reached a point that even non-Arabs are deciding not to serve, like the Yesh Gvul movement, whose members say that they are willing to serve inside Israel but not in the Occupied Territories.

I did not need the intifada to make me aware of this possibility, as I decided a long time ago not to serve in the army. The Druze simply have not received equal treatment. If you go to any Druze village or any other Arab village, you will see that it has not changed in twenty years. Why should we give more than others but be in the same situation? Why should the state argue that the other "minorities" need not go to the army? For Muslims, for example, the argument is that we are in a state of war with their brothers and that it is not fair to expect them to take up arms. Why should that not be applied to me too? After all, we are all Arabs. Why should a Druze be placed opposite his brother from Syria or Lebanon, which happened during the Lebanese War. Why should we accept such a thing?

PART 3

WOMEN

Dr. Lily Moed and Judy Blanc

In protesting the Occupation and calling for peace, Israeli women have emerged as a vibrant and creative public. Those who connected issues of women's liberation with national liberation joined forces with those who feared for their sons and husbands serving in the Occupied Territories. Whereas women often formed the core of mixed men's and women's peace and protest groups, women also developed their own organizational frameworks. Groups like the Women in Black, who dress in black and meet each Friday afternoon in central Jerusalem for a silent vigil, have sustained a high level of activism throughout the intifada. Meeting often with their Palestinian women counterparts in the Occupied Territories, these women are in the forefront of the struggle for peace and a just settlement of the conflict.

We spoke with Dr. Lily Moed and Judy Blanc, both long-time political activists and among the founders of SHANI — Israeli Women against the Occupation.

Editors: How do you think the intifada has clarified the concept of justice for Israeli society?

Judy: I am not sure that it has clarified the concept, but it has put the question on the agenda in whatever confused form it exists. Certainly among Jews, the contradiction between a Jewish state and democratic values, a state that gives rights to one people over another, is something that people can see as an issue now, and this is an important step forward. Do people, therefore, vote for justice? Have they moved forward in their thinking? I am not sure.

There has been a growth in sentiment for what we would call a two-states solution. Is this a result of a sharpened sense of justice? To some degree yes, but not in the abstract sense, not in the sense that people are examining their measure and applying it to society. They recognize now that Palestinians are a people. The antijustice forces are clearly trying to dehumanize the enemy. Since the outbreak of the intifada, though, there has been some progress on this level.

In our groups we do not center our discussions on this issue of justice. I think that in the case of the intifada, liberal circles and beyond have been raised to a new level of consciousness. This has certainly been the case on human rights issues. I have been referring up to now to justice on the national level — "Shalom tsodek," a just peace. I was not referring to the dreadful abuses. The fact that these represent a lack of justice is overwhelmed by the fact that they represent a lack of humanity. I think that this has hit people on that level more than as an insult to their sense of justice. The direction is not to sharpen their sense of justice but to focus on treatment of Palestinians as individuals. Clearly many of these human rights violations, such as imprisonment without trial, are stated within the context of the judicial system.

Those who say, "End the Occupation" — the Women in Black, for instance — have been influenced by the public to see that unless there is an end to the Occupation, there will be no end to both human rights violations and terrorist responses. That question has been sharpened, although not necessarily translated into your language — the language of justice. But the link has been made that the rebellion will continue so long as there are occupiers (that is, oppressors) and occupied.

Lily: Judy and I had just met on a bus to a Yesh Gvul demonstration when we discussed whether there was room for a women's peace group. That is how we began. On that bus we fixed a meeting, we met, and SHANI took off. In retrospect it is quite remarkable. From that day we started to meet once every two weeks, and since then we have been probably the most consistent, ongoing women's peace group in the country. We have regular public meetings. It grew with a core group of women, half social activists and half feminists, and then we brought in women who were yet unpoliticized. Our concern was the intifada. For me personally, the intifada did not highlight questions of justice, for I was in the struggle against the Occupation before the intifada. For me it was just a continuation.

As I see its effect on the public and its version of justice, I think that the intifada has highlighted the gross fact of the two systems of justice in this country — one for Jew, and another for Arab. As for the people I encounter on vigils or within my daughter's ultra-Orthodox community or just out there, I could say that justice is not an issue for them. Security has to be maintained for the Jews at any cost. I view this as an emotional, not a rational, reaction to the situation here, especially since the beginning of the intifada. If they are on the side of "we must maintain security," then anything that has to be done must be done; if that includes brutality, so be it.

Most societies that call themselves democratic do not want to educate their public as to what justice really means. So we have a fairly irrational and uneducated public, which has accepted whatever the mass media have given them in terms of the viewpoint of the government, which is "security at all costs." The government understands that this total lack of justice does not bring security, but since we have an uneducated public, you can sell them anything. At this point many people are very confused. Even the relatively educated public that likes to think of itself as liberal, the public that adheres to a system of justice, is in conflict. Strategically, those are the people that we have to go for first, to move them along, because they are troubled about justice and the reality of Israeli policy and what they are doing during the intifada.

Eds.: Both of you are working within the context of a group. Could you say something about how this group of women is working on some of these issues?

Lily: When we first began, we attracted women on the basis of their outrage during the early stages of the intifada. I would say that some of the women we got were not social activists. We got some of what we might call "average people" who were just emotionally reacting. But as we educated them, they could fit together the cognitive and the emotional, and it became what we now have — a solid core of women who attend meetings and are active with us. This is one subgroup.

Another subgroup has been the feminists. Some of these have been very concerned about justice for Palestinians and could intellectually link the whole notion of oppression of women and oppression of Palestinians in terms of power relationships. That whole thing was unjust. But then some of the feminists were strong nationalists, Zionists. Many of those women are now very active in organizing. These are women who have developed a new consciousness about the Palestinian situation, and it was the intifada that helped them on the way. This group is now working against the Occupation. They had not been involved in the peace movement but had been very involved in the women's movement. Some of them are far left feminists who, until two or three years ago, were left untouched by this issue of the Palestinians, which they saw as a distraction to their work of gaining equality for women in Israel. It is interesting that many of these women are now on the peace and justice bandwagon. Since the intifada something clicked for them.

Judy: The women were primarily interested in meeting Palestinians. In our first meeting I gave some background on the Palestinian women's organization, and the very next meeting we had our first meeting with a Palestinian woman. That was the hallmark of SHANI in the beginning — meeting with Palestinian women in our homes first, before the public meetings. Within the first weeks we had organized a demonstration in connection with women prisoners.

Lily: Israeli women have had a powerful desire to meet with Palestinians. Having worked here for some years before the intifada and having been aware of the segregation between the two societies, I was still amazed at how little Israeli women know. Some women had never been across to East Jerusalem. On our trip to Ramallah, there were people who had lived here all their lives but had never been to a Palestinian city.

Judy: This need to meet Palestinians was a very complex need.

Lily: Well, there was simple curiosity. Suddenly there is an uprising and everyone is asking: "Who are these people? What are they like? What do they want?" The intifada put the Palestinians on the front page and moved them into the consciousness of Israelis. Although the Occupation was never benign in terms of treatment of the Palestinians, it was benign in the sense that the Occupation just rolled along for the Israelis. For us as a women's group it was therefore natural to ask: "Who are these Palestinian women? Can we meet them?" We had a marvelous attendance at these meetings. Whenever we had a Palestinian speaker, we packed the room; whenever we did not have a Palestinian speaker, we got perhaps half the attendance. It became evident that this was the most important thing that we were doing.

Eds.: Could you explain more clearly the interwovenness of injustice against women in this society and oppression of Palestinians.

Lily: I'll speak for myself and people I know. We have a power structure where there is institutional oppression, where the institutions discriminate against women — as they do in jobs and in power sharing on the governmental level. For example, we only have ten representatives in the Knesset. This is paralleled by the Palestinian case and how the Israeli government deals with it. It is not the same system, of course, but the analogy relates to power relations. Once I realize that the system of power is so warped that it can affect me as a woman and a Palestinian, as it does in this situation, then to gain equality for myself I have to put an end to that kind of power relation. I have to end this system that has the capability of discriminating in this way.

Judy: Lily and I differ on this. Lily is a particularly thoughtful and thorough feminist radical. I think that there are few like her. I do not think, though, that the majority of women in the organized women's movement would make such a connection. I do not agree that there is a valid link between the oppression of women and the oppression of Palestinians. We see a variety of systems that are more or less democratic, and the position of women does not vary according to how democratic the system is. I do not see that the position of women has gotten worse as a consequence of increased state exclusivity.

Eds.: What is startling about the intifada, though, is that women have emerged so forcefully in both the Israeli and the Palestinian protest movements that this is an inseparable phenomenon of the intifada. Where is this coming from?

Judy: I do not think that it comes from a sharper sense of their oppression. On the Israeli side, part of this is because the men are serving in the army and the women are expressing, in their concern and involvement, the contradictions that the men are facing but cannot express.

Lily: I have a different analysis. I think that the outward reason for the behavior of women might be that their men are in the army. But I also believe that somewhere at some subconscious level there is an intuitiveness about their oppression. I do not think that it is only because their men are in the army and that in this case they have more opportunity to maneuver, to protest and be more active. I think it is touching something that is very particular to their own oppression. They might not be able to articulate this, but somewhere in the emotionality of women toward the intifada, toward the brutality and injustice, there was a trigger that led women to see that something in that brutality relates to them. This is not a perfect parallel, for the oppression of Palestinians is not the same as the oppression of women in society. The similarities in the discrimination and oppression are structural, not connected to content.

Judy: What I was objecting to was the intellectual linkage. I think the linkage is the one made in the Bible, in the statement "You were strangers." Women respond on the level of this most remarkable phrase in the Bible. The linkage is between being strangers in the Land of Egypt and the commandment not to oppress others.

Lily: The similarity is in experience. They beat up on Palestinians, and women have an experience of being battered. Both have no access to power. Women might not be able to articulate this connection, but this is where the intuitiveness stems from.

Eds.: Where did your activism come from?

Lily: I come from a radical mother. I grew up in a socialist, Yiddish culture. I know no other life.

Judy: I was radicalized at university. Probably World War II contributed to that. Both of us arrived at the intifada as radicals.

Dr. Suha Hindiyye

Women's committees have played an essential role in the conscientization of the Palestinian masses. These committees have promoted the women's struggle alongside national liberation, fighting to secure the gains made by women for the future state. Women have found themselves at the front in this uprising as the soldiers invade their homes regularly, seeking the activist youth. Mothers have taken to the street to defend their sons and daughters from the Occupation soldiers and have found themselves as sole breadwinners when their husbands have been killed or detained. The women's committees prepare Palestinian women for a better future, free of all structures of oppression.

We spoke with Dr. Suha Hindiyye, a Jerusalem sociologist on the staff of the Women's Action Committees.

Editors: What has the intifada done to clarify for you the issues of justice?

Suha: The intifada has brought to the surface the unjust measures perpetrated by the Israeli authorities: land confiscation, water usage restriction, house demolitions, deportation, administrative detention, even in respect to education and health. The intifada is a just struggle, and I do not think it will stop before justice is achieved, in accordance with our rights that have been denied us for the past twenty-two years, or even forty years.

Eds.: Can you explain how you came to this clear enunciation of these concerns for justice?

Suha: Although I have not suffered from these repressive measures personally, living in East Jerusalem and coming from a middle-class family, still walking in the streets here, in East Jerusalem or wherever I go in the West Bank or Gaza Strip, they are visible everywhere: the army patrols, the checkpoints, being humiliated at a checkpost, having to show your ID card, travelling through Lyd Airport and being searched since we are Palestinians and are holding a special travel document. These experiences lead us to ask why they are doing these things to us. We are human beings.

What about the Palestinians who have been living in refugee camps for the past twenty or even forty years, who have been yearning for the days when they lived in their own villages, wherever they were, inside Israel proper? Or those who have been born during the Occupation, whose parents have told them what life used to be like. These people are not provided with even minimal services needed by a human being. Surely you have been into refugee camps in the Gaza Strip and the West Bank, and you have seen the conditions there. There is no proper sewage system (if it exists at all), no sanitation, and yet the Israelis are saying to the world, "We are providing them with all these services." They are not giving any services. Instead they are turning those refugees into cheap labor power, exploiting them in factories. These workers experience the national oppression at the factory, getting lower salaries than Israeli workers do at the same job. The Israelis get not only higher salaries but also all the securities that workers should have. What about arrests, collective punishment, seizures from villages, tortures in prison? All these issues accumulated led to the intifada. Experiencing these repressive measures leads to an intifada. This is not the first intifada, but it is the first one where all social strata, spread demographically all over the Occupied Territories, find together that they can no longer tolerate the situation.

Eds.: How would you say that growing up as a woman in Jerusalem has affected some of the work that you are doing today?

Suha: In 1967 I was eighteen or nineteen and I remember very well what happened then, how we were occupied, the fears we had as Palestinians — irrespective of my being a woman. Even before the Occupation, I started noticing how I was brought up differently from the male members in the family. Already then I began to experience injustice, knowing that these are the social traditions that a woman must suffer under. I was given some freedom, although it stops at a certain point. The freedom of the male members of the family does not stop at this same point. So I started to feel that injustice was being practiced against me and against women in general.

By the early 1970s I became involved in voluntary work. A group of Palestinians — petit bourgeois, some educated abroad — wanted to do something. Where should we begin? A mixed group of men and women, we sat together discussing this issue, and so we began voluntary work in the refugee camps and within institutions like old age homes, trying to offer our help. Getting involved sharpened my views on justice and injustice. I realized that my people are not offered services by anybody, and that we have to start doing it. Eventually, through working myself as a teacher in government schools in the villages, I noticed further the injustice against women. Some of this injustice is internalized within women themselves. They were brought up like this, and they know nothing better. As Palestinians, men and women know that injustice has been done.

Eds.: You have mentioned that women in the villages and refugee camps have a stronger personality than city women. Was there an incident in your life that demonstrated this for you?

Suha: In 1982 I returned from Britain to do my fieldwork here for my thesis, which was on aspects of sharecropping and commercialization in the West Bank before 1967. This meant that I had to go into villages and talk with farmers, villagers, and landowners. In the back of my mind I had the idea that these would all be men. This is the way I was brought up. I went into one of the villages in the Hebron area. I said to a woman sitting there, "I would like to talk with your husband, or your brother, the farmer in the family." She said: "The farmer in the family? Look at my hands. I am the farmer here. My husband is in prison." I felt ashamed of myself. Why didn't I know that our women are working in agriculture, even though I used to see them going to work the land? And so I interviewed that woman. This was not the beginning of a new perception, but it was certainly a sharpening. It sharpened even more my vision of women as having potential but having been denied the actualization of this potential. In Britain, during further studies, I got to know about feminist issues from a Western point of view.

Eds.: How would your thesis be different if you were doing it now during the intifada?

Suha: As a Palestinian and a woman, if I returned to do my thesis again, it would focus on women. Possibly I could focus on women and agriculture. All over the Third World, women work in agriculture. They are the heart, the core, the hands that do the work.

Eds.: What are you doing to promote justice?

Suha: Working at the Women's Action Committees, a grassroots women's organization, has sharpened my own awareness of injustice against women. We hold consciousness-raising sessions where women sit together and discuss the social, political, and psychological pressures exerted on them within the family and on a more general level. However, working in the offices and in the field itself, I notice that there is also indirect consciousness-raising by women just discussing issues while working. We are planning to hold a social-research course to recruit a cadre from the Women's Action Committees. We will discuss general issues — for example, a conference on women's liberation and national liberation. We are going to learn from these women, and they will learn from us. When the committees were established in 1978, women from Jerusalem and Ramallah went into the villages and camps. Going from house to house, they spoke with every woman inquiring about their needs and the needs of their families. Talking with these women, they discovered issues that bourgeois women would never have realized.

We do not act as an executive committee but as a grassroots organization. We work with women in different environments — villages, refugee camps, factories — trying to set up production programs and to bring women into production, which is very important as a first step toward women's social liberation, where they can earn an income. Women begin to understand the potential they have. They not only have been denied education but have been taught that they do not have this potential. Through these projects they have begun to realize such potential.

Orna Sasson-Levi

The intifada led to a surge in protest activity among Israeli Jews who were appalled by the Occupation. Many Israelis began to question profoundly, and the sacred national myths began to crumble. Some of those who recognized the severe injustice inherent in the Occupation were challenged to search further. They began to realize that the call to justice extended beyond the problem of the Occupied Territories. Israeli intellectuals began to uncover the dynamics that had led to the creation of the State of Israel itself, the traumatic circumstances of the

War of Independence in 1948 and the subsequent establishment of a Jewish state and displacement of Palestinian Arabs. These activists realized that although the call for peace and a two-states solution were the urgent issues of today, tomorrow Israel would have to deal with the question of equality for all its citizens, Jews and Palestinian Arabs who live within its borders.

We spoke with Orna Sasson-Levi, a sociologist and peace activist.

Editors: How did you become politically aware?

Orna: During my first year of university studies I met an Arab from Galilee. I said to myself very clearly: There are Arabs here, and I have to get to know them. It is the only chance in my life to get to know them on an equal basis. You might say that I arrived at this point with some sense of justice because out of a class of three hundred, I was the only one who made the attempt to get to know them. But back then I did not feel that it had anything to do with justice. Then they were people who lived with us all this time, and I had never met them. And now they were sitting with me in the same class, and so I had to get to know them.

I was very lucky when Muhammad, an Arab student, turned around to me and asked me for a book. We started talking and became close friends. The process of feeling comfortable with one another took a while, as we talked about more and more things between us. This was really like discovering a new world. Right here, under my nose, there was a whole world that existed, and I never knew about it. Here was a people that was different. They have a different culture, they talk differently, they live differently, they think differently — and it was interesting. Then I joined a Jewish-Arab students' dialogue group. We started talking more about things, and simultaneously I started doing my academic work on Israeli Arabs. So it was a combination of getting to know them as people and getting to know them academically. During my third year of studies, when I had almost completed my B.A., I was the facilitator of this Jewish-Arab group together with Muhammad.

I come from a very political, leftist family, but I myself was never political. I was never very interested and never had very clear ideas or opinions about what was right and what was wrong, neither here in Israel nor in the world. I was not aware politically. This whole voyage of discovery was my own political self-discovery. It was very independent. None of my friends was interested in the Jewish-Arab group. My husband was not interested, and even Muhammad was not interested in the beginning. It was something completely my own. This third year was a turning point.

When Muhammad and I were chosen to be the facilitators of this group, we went to a two-day seminar for people who were supposed to be moderators of groups like these. It was an enormous affair with about one hundred participants. In trying to put my finger on the turning point for me, I realize that two things happened at the same time. I realized then that just by coming here at the beginning of the century, we Jews had begun to do injustice to the Arabs who lived here, taking their land and everything that that implies. At the same time, I realized that I am standing in this conflict as a Jew, as an Ashkenazi, as a woman, and as a member of a kibbutz. In that seminar they tried to put us down very much. That seminar was very pro-Palestinian, and the facilitator of the seminar was very much opposed to members of the kibbutzim. Now I no longer identify myself as a kibbutz member, but then I was only five years out of the kibbutz and very much identified as a kibbutz member. There was no option in that room of being a Zionist. The thought of being an Ashkenazi kibbutz member was even worse. I stood up to oppose this facilitator and said, "You are talking against discrimination and against stereotyping people, but you are stigmatizing me."

I came back from that seminar and said to my father, and I remember it very clearly even though this is six or seven years ago, "The way I see it, we were not guilty of injustice in 1967, but Zionism from the beginning was committing injustice toward the Arabs." He answered: "Of course, from the beginning we were doing injustice, and we should try to do this as little as possible. We had no other choice then, as a Jewish state in desperate need, and it happened at the cost of another people. Now we have to try to minimize this injustice." That conversation changed my point of view.

For many Israelis to see Zionism as the original sin is very difficult. It is very revolutionary for me to say this to myself. In contrast, it makes it easier to live here. For me, it made me more peaceful with myself. I see that Zionism is the original sin, but I was born into an existing state, after the establishment of the State of Israel. A certain Israeli people exists, and I was born into this people. I am not that Jewish, but I am very Israeli. It is clear to me that this is the only place in the world where I could ever live. Therefore there is no good reason to commit more sins in order to expunge the original sin. We can only look forward to see how we can minimize this problem.

Eds.: When you talk about Zionism as the original sin, what exactly are you referring to?

Orna: At this very period I was working on some research, trying to find out why the Arab villages inside Israel were not urbanized as they should have been. They are the size of cities, but they have the character of villages. The findings clearly reveal discrimination on the part of the Israeli government. The Israeli government does not give budgets for streets, industry, sewage, or other basic needs. So when I say we must correct the original sin, I mean making them equal citizens. That is the very basic thing. Before I can talk of the Jewish Right of Return, I must talk about equality. There is discrimination against people in accepting applicants to schools, to jobs, and to other places.

I was talking recently to an Arab friend who was found guilty of contact with a hostile organization. He was sentenced to four months of community service, which he has just completed. Now there is nothing he can do. He cannot teach because to be a teacher he must go through security checks. He said that maybe he would buy a taxi, but to do that, he needs a certificate to prove that he has no criminal record. Of course, he cannot be accepted to law school now, and he cannot be a doctor. If he wants, he can study to be an engineer. He can study for four years, but then he will not find a job because all the industry is military. So what can he do? People like him are completely locked out. They have nowhere to go.

Personally I could live in a state that is not Jewish, to enable Palestinians to identify with the state. The state would be Israeli but not Jewish. I am not suggesting this as a solution, because I know that I am not representative. For me, if they changed the flag and the anthem tomorrow, it would be no problem. I would not mind if there was no flag at all. If they switched the menorah and the Star of David for some other Mediterranean symbol, I would have no problems with it.

Eds.: What you are saying is radical, compared with what much of the Israeli left says, namely, that maximal justice would be a state for the Palestinians in the Occupied Territories.

Orna: I think after the establishment of a Palestinian state, it will be worse for the Israeli Arabs. The establishment of the state will provide new legitimation for discrimination against the Arabs in Israel because then people will say: "If you like it here, welcome. But if you do not like being a second-class citizen, you have your own country; go there. If you do not go there, do not complain; if you want to stay here, do not complain." So I think that the situation within Israel is as problematic as the situation between Israel and the Territories. Solving only the problem of the Territories will not solve the problem of the Israeli Arabs. It will not make us a democracy again. As long as we have seven hundred thousand second-class citizens, we cannot define ourselves as a democracy.

During the years I was active in coexistence projects, I felt I was doing all I could. There are in fact three points that I would like to mention concerning this. First, there is my feeling of helplessness concerning the problem of the Israeli Arabs. Second, there is my disillusionment with what is done concerning the Israeli Arabs. Third, there is the intifada and what it did to me. About the helplessness, there is not much to be said. The problems that I have been talking about have to be solved at the government level. The budget issues are governmental. Possibly the social discrimination could be addressed by education. I feel very helpless when I look at the situation. The state has to provide both money and legitimacy to ensure that they are equal citizens.

Concerning my disillusionment about what is done now between Jews and Arabs in Israel, after I had gained certain awareness and insight, I started to work in a Jewish-Arab project in the Van Leer Institute. I led Jewish-Arab seminars and encounter groups. I led a lengthy seminar for Jews who work in youth movements. I was also working on a Jewish curriculum for fourth and sixth grades. During the time I was working in Van Leer, we had a course there for group facilitators. There it became clear that the Jews and the Arabs among the facilitators see the group and the work in completely different terms. The Jews mostly see the work as psychological. By working on inhibitions, fears, stereotypes, and anxieties, Jews and Arabs will change and they will treat each other better. The Arabs, on the other hand, see the work as political. They use the meeting as a platform to say out loud that they are discriminated against, thinking the Jews will change their minds and see the real situation. They are working all the time on two different levels. If you work on the political level within the group, then the only thing achieved is that the Jews feel more and more guilty, but nothing else emerges. They feel guilty, which causes resentment, and they get angry. In the end they hate the Arabs more than they did in the beginning. They have more stereotypes than they had in the beginning. So there is no use working only on the political level in the group.

But to work only on the psychological level, I feel, is a big lie. If we talk about justice, that is doing an injustice. When we work on the psychological level, we are in fact saying that we are all equal. We are saying that we here in this room, Jews and Arabs, are all equal because we have the same psychological make-up. We all have fears, and those fears are all the same; it does not matter if my fears are from the Holocaust, and the Arab's fears are from 1948; we all have the same fears.

Another disillusionment was the realization that all the institutions that work for Jewish-Arab coexistence are part of the establishment as well. They are all very Jewish, and they are all playing the game in one way or another. Maybe there is no way of doing anything equal in this state. Even where I work, where we were labelled as extreme leftists, we were fifteen Jews and one Arab. There was a token Arab. It was never even close to 50-50. When the token Arab would leave, we would immediately have to find a replacement. When I pointed out to the director that we should aspire to a 50-50 balance if this was to be truly a Jewish-Arab project, he responded: "But I am always looking for young educated Arabs. If you know anyone, please send him to me." As if we did not know anyone! As if hundreds of educated Arabs were not working in black labor!

The initial days of the intifada were unusually difficult for me. During the first weeks we had a friend who came back from reserve duty in Gaza. He came back with horrible stories about what "our" soldiers were doing to the people of Gaza. Three weeks later someone else came back, and he had terrible stories too. He told of people taken to a garbage dump where they had their hands and legs broken; they were tied up and then left there. That was only one of his stories. He was a medic, and they did not allow him to take care of the people. He tried, together with two other soldiers from his unit, to get to a member of the Knesset to tell him everything. At first he wanted to go to the papers, so they brought the regional commander to talk to the soldiers so that they would not tell anyone what had happened. For me that was the first sign of the police state. He got scared. He was not a political person, just very humane. So he agreed to talk to a member of Knesset instead of the press. At least that way he could get the information out. The morning he went out to talk to Knesset member Ran Cohen, the military police came to his home and detained him for a day. I do not know if you can even understand how terrible this story is. That means that they followed him even when he had completed his reserve duty. He was not a free civilian. I heard more stories like this one. People were even expelled from their units.

This is my home, and it is frightening and difficult to accept. When that story occurred at the beginning of the intifada, there was a common feeling that something must be done. That was one of the few times that I did not feel like a minority. Then the protest group called The 21st Year was organized, and I got involved. I felt something was being done, and with the intifada the question of the Occupation became most urgent. The main feeling was that these soldiers are doing this in my name, and I do not want to be a partner to it. What they are doing is indeed unjust, but it is even more unjust that they do it in my name. They pollute me. To purify myself I have to work against it. I cannot say that I am apolitical, therefore it is not done in my name, or that I am pro-Palestinian, so it is not in my name. No, as long as I am a Jewish Israeli, it is done in my name. I have to work against it as long as it is done because I will always be an Israeli.

In the beginning the whole of Israeli society was shocked. People were mobilized then on the conscience level. Everything focused around the issue of conscience. We had house meetings here in our home, and people were prepared to talk night after night after night, talking to more and more people about what should be done, about what could be done. In the beginning I gave hours and hours to this issue. For six months that is all I did, even though I had a six-month-old baby at the time. I devoted five or six hours every day to The 21st Year in addition to holding down a job and looking after my children. I had a feeling that everyone was prepared to sacrifice in order to keep a clean conscience. But now people have gotten used to it. It makes me depressed to think about it.

Eds.: How can public opinion in Israel be influenced?

Orna: My only example is the war in Lebanon. Public opinion changed only after we suffered a lot. After six hundred men were killed, Israeli society started panicking. You could feel the panic; it was very tangible. It was not like people going through a war, which is dangerous but within a week or month is over. It was an ongoing thing. People were constantly being called to reserve duty, and every day someone was being killed. Maybe it was the same during the War of Attrition. It was very scary when someone went to Lebanon. My husband went twice, and I begged him to refuse. I begged him mostly because I preferred that he sit in jail rather than go to Lebanon. It would have been safer. Everyone knew someone who was killed. Everyone knew families who suffered. There was such fear everywhere. In the end there was a consensus. When Peres finally decided on withdrawal, there was no objection whatsoever. There was complete agreement.

For the first time since 1967, the balance of losses and gains concerning the Territories is tipping toward losses for Israel. Only when it tips drastically to the side of the losses will something change. Adaptation processes are already developing to make sure that we do not lose anything from the new situation. These adaptation processes include getting used to the numbers of Palestinians killed so that that fact no longer arouses one to action. I feel terrible that I do not know how many Palestinians were killed today.

Dr. Mariam Mar'i

Palestinians who have lived within Israel since 1948 as Israeli citizens serve as a convergence point of the conflict. During the intifada these Palestinians have had to tread the delicate tightrope between their sense of identification with their people in the Occupied Territories and their loyalty as citizens to the State of Israel. They have expressed themselves in full solidarity with their compatriots in the West Bank and Gaza Strip, giving humanitarian assistance wherever possible, and have used the political possibilities available to them as Israeli citizens to protest the policies of the Israeli government. With deep knowledge of both parties to the conflict, they may one day serve as a bridge to understanding.

We spoke with Dr. Mariam Mar'i, a Haifa educator, an instructor at Haifa University, and director of a pedagogical center in Acre. She is also a member of various Jewish-Arab groups for coexistence.

Mariam: I am a woman, a Palestinian, and an Israeli; I am a member of a national minority. We suffer from internal conflicts because of the struggle to find some kind of harmony among these various identities. This is my whole story.

As a child, I went with my mother and my whole family to Lebanon in 1948. We lived there for three years during my early childhood. I did not know my father until we returned, and then I was already five years old. My brothers, uncles, and cousins were the males I knew, and they served as father substitutes. I remember the day when we returned to where we had lived. We were a large extended family with cousins and their children, and we all lived in the same house. In that house there was no privacy. Women lived in one room, men in another, and children in a third. The sense of belonging was quite different from that common in the nuclear family.

Much of the time was spent waiting for something to happen. The adults had waited to return to Palestine, and I had waited to see my father again. But even after our return, the happiness did not last long, since the family was still divided: three of my brothers were left in Lebanon as refugees because the Israeli law did not permit the return of men over the age of sixteen. My sisters were also prevented from returning because they were married and therefore independent. Those who returned were my mother, my younger sisters, and one brother. My first fifteen years were filled with pain. My mother wept constantly. She longed to see her sons and daughters and was desperate for information about them. At that time there was no process of national Palestinian education in Israel.

The events that happened to my family were behind my own national awareness and slow process of awakening. Whenever we talked about Palestine, we lowered our voices. Whenever we were critical of what was going on around us, we made sure that it remained within the family. We were controlled by fear and a sense of instability. We continued to wait for those who were outside to return. This is the atmosphere in which I was raised. I felt different from the other children, and thus, early on, I noted the difference between Palestinian and Jewish children. The Jews were our occupiers; they took our land and came and went as they pleased. The only thing we had left was waiting for Palestine.

In our schools there was no mention of the history of Palestine. The educational curriculum was devoid of anything that related directly to us. We were taught grammar, arithmetic, poetry from all over the world, love poems and poems about nature. But all of this had no connection with what was burning inside us. No one could give us answers. There was no press to write about our story and no radio stations to tell us what was really going on. You live, but you feel that you are confined to a small hole and that no one knows about you and your suffering and tragedy. I was driven by a sense that I needed to be educated in order to wrestle with the things around me.

The Arab radio stations outside began broadcasting the news to us, and this coincided with the Nasser period, the revolution in Egypt, the *coup d'état* in Syria, and the revolutions in Iraq and Algeria. This suddenly taught us to identify as Arabs, not just as individuals. Thus I realized that I was an Arab; after 1967 the Palestinian identity came into prominence. The feeling of Arab nationalism was most important because we believed that the resolution of the Palestine problem would be through the auspices of Arab nationalism. We were deeply disappointed in 1967 when we realized that belonging to the Arab nation was insufficient. We realized that the solution to our problem would not be coming from the outside but that we as Palestinians needed to do something. My generation was the first one that began to see itself as Palestinian. I am not an Israeli Arab or even an Arab living under Israeli rule. I am a Palestinian living in Israel.

Editors: As a Palestinian woman, what do you propose to Israeli women in order to face a common, just, and peaceful future?

Mariam: As women, we have a great role to play. We are still suffering in the larger human society. As women, we are still struggling for our freedom and our right to be a part of the decision-making process. As women, we do understand the need for struggle to achieve our ambitions. The Palestinian people ask for peace, even if they use other means at times. These means are solely to achieve an end, and war is not a goal in itself. Human beings have constructive and destructive potential, but eventually the constructive could control the destructive. The ultimate ambition of the Palestinians is to reach peace. Women are the most important group who can understand this way.

Israeli women have not achieved their own independence and therefore live under similar circumstances. The Israeli woman who understands her own situation, who can detach herself from her particular personal experience, could understand the Palestinian experience, and eventually she would be a positive element in supporting the Palestinian peace process.

In my understanding, peace is reached between two enemies. Real peace can be achieved only between two parties who have the feeling of equality and self-respect. When I feel self-respect and confidence, then I reflect this in my behavior with others, and I will be ready to make peace. Before the intifada the Palestinians did not feel that they had the self-confidence or sense of empowerment needed to propose a peace plan. This period has given Palestinians a sense of restoring their own dignity.

Look at the experience of women. When women were weak and self-effacing, they perceived men as their primary enemy. They saw men as the source of authority, power, oppression, and control, and they acted out of weakness and fear. But when women began to feel that they had values of their own, their war was no longer with men. Rather, they sought to join with men to build a better society for both.

We are partners with men in this life, as they are our children, our fathers, our brothers, and we should love them. They are no longer our enemies, although it took us quite some time to understand this. This is applicable also to the issue of national conflict. Palestinians who have restored their self-confidence and dignity, their sense of achieving and of identity, no longer see Israelis as the enemy. The challenge is now to continue the process, not against, but with the others.

Unfortunately the peace movements within Israel suffer from a lack of credibility among their own people. Those who talk about peace are labelled as pro-Palestinian and therefore lose their effective role in Israeli society. These peace movements are not paying enough attention to their own society. Instead of focusing their own attention inside Israel, they are directing all their attention to the Palestinians who support peace to extract more and more concessions from them. Because they do not work enough within the Israeli camp, they have little influence and therefore they feel embittered. They see themselves as caught in the middle, for they are not identified with either side. They have lost their credibility in both camps and therefore cannot move ahead. They have good intentions and want to change, but they are up against a strong dam wall. They face a strong offensive from the Israelis, and the Palestinians cannot offer them further concessions.

Prof. Naomi Hazan

Israelis have been overwhelmed by events since the intifada began. The age of innocence has passed, and many Israelis realize that it cannot be recaptured. Israeli intellectuals and academics are faced with the difficult task of analyzing what has happened, what went wrong. Many of these academics have courageously taken up the challenge. Deeply committed to confronting injustice and promoting peace, academics and intellectuals have been active on many fronts.

We spoke with Prof. Naomi Hazan, a senior lecturer in political science and African studies at the Hebrew University of Jerusalem.

Editors: How has the intifada affected Israeli society, and how do you think it has focused issues of justice?

Naomi: The first question is, of course, how one defines justice. My tendency is to think of it more in political terms than in legal or moral terms. Justice, first, means a certain degree of self-determination, the ability to make decisions for oneself. The removal of that ability from any people is, almost by definition, unjust. We find that situation most prominently in classic colonial situations or in highly authoritarian regimes where people are not sufficiently free to determine the course of their own social actions. This is very closely linked in my mind to the element of participation and representation. When we talk about self-determination, we are talking about the capacity to participate relatively freely in the making of decisions. That involves some form of delegation in modern societies, which means equitable representation also. Any situation that removes these basic features is extraordinarily problematic and creates or exacerbates inequalities in society.

I always thought that the Occupation was, by definition, unjust. It lacked any of the basic components that I consider to be a foundation for the creation of a just society. I have always equated the Occupation with a latter-day colonial situation in most senses because I think the colonial situations are unjust.

Your immediate question was how the intifada has affected that, and I have to say that in my own personal case it has more confirmed than affected. The imposition of a colonial situation breeds the roots for anticolonialism. The intifada, in this context, is in many respects a struggle for national liberation, an anticolonial struggle. It is, to a certain extent, different because of the proximity between the colonized and the colonizer, and that creates different forms of tension than would exist in places like colonial Nigeria or colonial Kenya, where there was a great distance between the white colonial administrators and the bulk of the population. This raises the issues of confrontation concerning national identity and boundaries. This does not exist in a classic colonial situation. Obviously the best comparisons, if you see the most intractable problems in the world today, are those that have these features in common, like Northern Ireland. There too the matter of proximity and the issue of national identity coincide.

I want to talk on a more personal level as an Israeli. I have had difficulty with any analysis of Zionism in the classic sense, which does not see the Zionist movement in terms of a national liberation movement of the Jewish people. Historically, Zionism makes sense within that kind of context. This is a basic pillar for me regarding the legitimacy of the State of Israel. Without the notion of Zionism as a national liberation movement — that if we have the right, then obviously other national liberations have the same right — there is nothing much to discuss. That is, Israelis should recognize that their collective self-determination is an imperative that demands that they recognize the need for the collective self-determination of others. Otherwise we do not have a justification on which we can base what we are.

Demographically, the vast majority of the citizens of Israel within the Green Line are of Third World origin. But the original kernel of the citizens of the state was of European derivation. Essentially what you had was a bunch of Polish chicken farmers coming with ideas, Bolshevik in structure with highfalutin democratic content, underwritten by socialist-utopian ideals. It is very difficult to sustain this combination of ideas over a long period, especially in conditions of conflict. The combination is neither adaptive nor responsive to reality. What has followed is a very serious deflation of power within political society over the past decade. The only way I can conceive of Israel is as a democratic state with a Jewish majority. A democratic state should ensure representation, equal allocation, equitable allocation of resources, and so forth, because I think that all we have talked about is really a prelude to the kinds of issues that are going to confront us in the twenty-first century: basic issues of equity and equality. This relates to relations among the various citizens of the state, Jewish and non-Jewish.

Eds.: What advantages are there for the peace and justice process if we proceed with a Third World model?

Naomi: You need some optimism at this stage of the game. There is no decolonization process that has not succeeded in the Third World. Some have been very disruptive, cruel, and inhumane. But one of the most successful political processes of the twentieth century is decolonization. The last of the old colonial systems — Namibia — has achieved independence now, after a very protracted process. So here too one has to assume that there are certain inexorable processes at work. Let me put it in context. It is quite clear now that there cannot be peace unless there is justice in my terms, which involve self-determination, participation, and representation. To divorce the issues is ridiculous. If one removes the Palestinian issue from the Arab-Israeli conflict, then one is missing the whole point, and that is why peace without addressing the Palestinian issue is ludicrous. If one addresses the Palestinian issue as it relates to the colonial context, then any resolution of the Palestinian issue requires self-determination. Therefore, there can be no peace if there is no justice.

The affirming thing is that these processes are very clear for somebody looking from the outside. It is much more difficult if you are caught up in the "day-to-dayism" of the Occupation, and then it appears that it gets worse all the time. But the truth of the matter is that the direction of the processes is clear and the issues are not really serious analytic issues at this junction. The issues are more strategic: How long is it going to take? Who is going to do it? How is it going to be done? And — the human issue — how many people are going to suffer in the process? Anybody who envisions this area in the twenty-first century without Palestinian self-determination and sovereignty, at least in its initial stage, is not mustering the tools that are available from a Third World perspective. Things are definitely moving. I can illustrate that very clearly just from a reading of the intifada. Before the intifada, the discussion of the PLO as a legitimate partner was considered ridiculous, taboo, beyond the consensus. Now, however, everybody recognizes that the core of the debate concerns the Palestinian state. Even the racism that is rampant on the far right is a reaction to the understanding that the processes are going in a certain direction. Venal kinds of solutions, like transferring the Palestinians, are nevertheless advancing the issue of Palestinian self-determination by rejecting it outright. They are not avoiding it entirely.

Eds.: Would you speak about the issue of collaborators within the decolonization context?

Naomi: Decolonization processes have very distinct phases and a very distinct dynamic. Part of the struggle is an open confrontation between the colonizer and the colonized. Usually it takes on a political form. When the political form does not work, it takes on military forms, and military forms usually breed social forms of confrontation, processes of institution building and distancing. Sometimes, when no solution is in sight, they take on communal forms, and in many respects, at least at the beginning of the intifada, there was this communal form of confrontation. But when we are at a very high level of escalation of the conflict (and it only happens in violent and protracted decolonization processes), the issue is not only the concrete form but also the symbolic form of confrontation. During the second year of the intifada the issue became not whether you can sustain this level of low-grade opposition (because it is sustainable for a long period), but the symbolic level. The real struggle is the struggle for control. Israel is playing the game of the politics of control of individual Palestinians. Palestinians, meanwhile, are using more and more sophisticated methods to avoid that control, not necessarily violent ones, often very subtle ones.

Now to your question of collaboration. In many respects Israel's policy can be understood in this context of the struggle for control.

You try to force your domination by linking each person, as much as possible, to some kind of administrator to increase dependence on Israel. For example, if you want a car license, you have to pay your taxes. The most important level of confrontation is not stone throwing, with all due respect to those involved, but Israel's effort to create bothersome and nerve-racking forms of bureaucratic and administrative dependence. To do that, it must penetrate and control the society that is resisting, and the method for doing so is by using collaborators. One of the great achievements of the intifada is the creation of a society that is not so permeable. The Palestinians are resisting, and the Israelis are trying to penetrate by bribing political prisoners, by drugs, by prostitution rings, and by other terrible means. To the extent that these sources of penetration are operating in this struggle for control, Palestinian autonomy and self-sufficiency are set back.

This is the struggle now. Israel is trying to control through collaboration, and Palestinians are trying to resist this control through the murder of collaborators. Let me add a fact to drive this point home. I always say to my students that violence, in the first instance in the anticolonial struggle, tends to be internalized, not externalized. Read Fanon on the subject. Take facts and figures: In the great Mau Mau movement in Kenya, between thirteen thousand and eighteen thousand blacks were killed; figures for whites range only from thirty-two to seventy-eight. This is indicative. The Israeli authorities are now saying, "How can you trust Palestinians if they are killing their own?" Well, they should go back to the history of Jewish society before the establishment of the State of Israel, when there were assassinations by certain Jewish underground movements who saw the worst offense as the offense of collaboration. We are talking about colonialism and domination and resistance to domination. Colonialism would not be possible without collaboration, and therefore it is perfectly logical that one of the first targets of any struggle is going to be those people who betray.

Eds.: Just as the issue of killing collaborators is being used to discredit the Palestinian leadership, religious resurgence is also being used in the same way, by stressing the Islamic component to the intifada. Can you analyze this in the same way?

Naomi: It is well known that Israel first promoted these Islamic movements. HAMAS (the Islamic resistance movement) was outlawed only a few months ago probably because it was nurtured by the Israeli authorities as a counterforce to the national movement. During the counterattack, the Israeli authorities seek to suggest that the real forces are not the national forces but rather the fundamentalist forces. Fundamentalist forces are almost by definition irrational. How can you deal with irrational forces? They are out for the destruction of the State of Israel and the creation of an Islamic state and God knows what else.

I want to flip your question though. I do not know of any nationalistic movement in protracted periods of struggle that has not undergone fragmentation. If I were looking from a Palestinian perspective, I would be a little concerned about this. The lack of tangible achievements lays the groundwork for the growth of fundamentalism, and its interests are parochial interests. Many of the Palestinians I know are worried precisely in those terms. You have some of the classic cases of fragmentation of national movements on an ethnic basis in places like South Africa today. How could they legalize the ANC? Hallelujah, after almost thirty years they did! But we also know that Inkatha of the Zulus is now a political force that cannot be ignored. Part of it is the politics of control, but part of it is the dynamics of internal splits in liberation movements, which the PLO has had its fair share of. But these splits have always been within the nationalist ideological spectrum; it's the parochial forms that constitute a serious threat to the nationalist coalition.

Eds.: Was there a turning point in your personal or academic life as a result of these insights?

Naomi: I cannot say that the intifada was an earth-shaking experience for me. If anything, I have started shifting some of my interests and research from Africa to Israel. Levels of involvement have risen because the situation demands it. It was very nice in the mid-1970s to sit back and write an article, but I do not think that any Israeli can afford to sit back and just write an academic paper now.

Eds.: You are involved in the women's political protest movement. Could you make some connection between the women's movement and the political situation?

Naomi: There has been a definite rise in political activism among Israeli women since the beginning of the intifada, and as a result several things are happening simultaneously. First, with the proliferation of peace and protest movements, the prominence of women in mixed groups has been very visible. In major demonstrations women are by far the majority. New groups have been formed, and women are very prominent in these mixed-gender groups. In addition, women's peace movements have sprung up. This began as early as 1982, when a group was formed called Mothers against Silence, but it lasted only two weeks before it was turned into Parents against Silence. It lost its feminine identity. Now you have an array of women's peace groups: Women in Black, Women for Political Prisoners, Women against Occupation, the Peace Cloth, and others. There is also a coalition of seven different groups — Women for Peace, generally known as the Coalition. At the same time, women, who are not very well represented in political parties, have moved into the extra-parliamentary sphere. This combination means a broadening of the ranks of those involved in women's peace activities, so you have the development of the Women's Network, which is another kind of wide coalition that encompasses what is now known as more radical women as well as women who have never been seen talking politics outside their living rooms.

Why all this activity? Some of the reasons are logical and obvious, and some are contradictory. We have done extensive research on why women have become involved and have gotten almost as many different answers as the people asked. I attribute to simple reasons great importance. The first reason is that many women feel much more comfortable expressing themselves in the protective confines of women's organizations rather than in general organizations. This is particularly true when it comes to political matters. In Israel there is almost a culture of nonparticipation of women in general political discussions. Women's organizations provide an outlet for what is perceived as a great need — to talk.

A second reason relates to perceptions of femininity. Two contradictory reasons relate to this factor. A whole group of women has been mobilized for political action precisely because they are feminist. Because they are feminists they connect issues of feminism with pacifism. They are the ones who make the almost one-to-one axiomatic correlation between feminism, nonviolence, and even pacifism. I think the intifada brought feminists out of their closets of feminism and put them into the political arena. They see the struggle against the Occupation as part of the struggle against gender stereotypes that suppress and subordinate women in Israeli society. These feminists have gotten their political act together.

But a third reason, which contradicts this, is that a lot of the intifada has to do with questions of what your son or husband is going to be doing or is doing during regular or reserve military service. Some of the women who are coming into the women's movement are coming in precisely as mothers and wives. In other words, they are taking the stereotype and they are politicizing it. Each of these two groups — feminist on the one hand, and mothers and wives on the other — is in evidence. This is also the source of a possible split in some of the movements. You get these two motives, and they are not coming from the same place. Those who are coming in as wives and mothers are very bourgeois in their personal lives. They are married, they have children, they spend a lot of time cooking. A lot of the feminists, however, are single, and their personal lifestyle is very different.

The nature of the intifada is very important. Unlike all of Israel's previous wars, except 1948, it does not involve tanks and planes. Israeli women know their place in real wars: the home front, where they are nurses, do laundry, cook, make sure that society is functioning "while the men are protecting the homeland." But the intifada is not that kind of confrontation; it is communal confrontation. There is no distance between the war front and the home front. It is only this functional and physical distance that allows for this separation on a gender basis in wartime. Women in this situation are as vulnerable, exposed, and as uncertain as men are. This is the first time that women are really a part, and they have to take a clear position because their roles are not predefined. I attribute great importance to the nature of the intifada and what it demands of women, who are coming to terms with what is going on.

Also, the themes that the intifada raises — self-determination, justice, freedom, equality — are all feminist themes. They resonate very well in women who feel that they have been somewhat exploited. When you consider the nature and the substance of the confrontation, it is not hard for women to make decisions and for these to be translated into activism of a peace and protest organization. Here the intifada has made a difference because this would not have happened without the intifada. Furthermore, the status of women plays a role. The deterioration in the status of women has raised consciousness as to the inequality between the sexes in Israel and has promoted a lot of women's interest groups. Where these existed before, they were co-opted. Now you have things like the Israel Women's Networks, battered women's shelters, groups advocating stricter sentencing for rape, and so on. The frameworks existed, and they were dealing with purely women's issues, but when the intifada came along, it was quite natural that some of this energy would be politicized.

I think that this is a part of a strategic change on the part of women. Activists now realize that women's issues must be mainstreamed, that there is a need to show a connection between these issues and the issues at the top of the national agenda. The obvious way to mainstream is to link women's issues with questions of war and peace. There is a small but very important kernel of women in the movement for whom this is a logical extension.

Another symbolic reason for the increase in women's protest activity is the very dominant political culture in this country. It has a hegemony, and it justifies the maintenance of a standing army for reasons of defense and survival. Evidently over the years there has developed a whole series of concepts that glorify the sensitive hero, who fights but does not want to fight, the reluctant hero who is always humane. This is the idea of the comrade in arms, solidarity, loyalty, and networking; these are all-important elements in this reigning symbolic structure. Women have generally been quiet in all this and pooh-poohed it. The intifada has raised interesting issues concerning this though, because women are not bound by the reigning paradigms. Therefore they may have more room to maneuver ideologically and symbolically as compared to their male counterparts because they do not have any vested interests in maintaining this particular set of reigning values. Possibly a women's peace counterculture is developing.

The next reason follows logically, and that is that women tend to be less dogmatic in their political beliefs. Women tend to be less convinced of their political positions, less emphatic, and as a result they are more open to listening to something that they had not heard before. I want to support this with a basic fact: two-thirds of the floating vote in Israel consists of women. This shows that in all probability there is a greater fluidity among women than among men. Finally all this is working. The women's peace movement has clearly grown during the intifada. The development of the mixed peace movements is completely erratic, but the women's movements are growing and attracting new adherents. Women are saying: "Why should I go with something that is erratic? I might as well go with something that is working." The more it works, the greater it attracts.

The women's movement has succeeded in maintaining long-term contact with Palestinian women. One of the reasons for the success of the movement is that it is maintaining a different type of dialogue. This is not a reason to get involved, but it is a reason why women stay. This maintenance of dialogue offers an interesting new model for Israeli-Palestinian relations. The fact that you are almost obliged to your Palestinian counterpart sustains activity. Women are very consistent and do not burn out. They do not opt out, and they exhibit an amazing perseverance. Women in Black is a perfect example; rain or shine, its members are there.

Dr. Jacqueline Sfeir

The intifada is about the future of Palestinian society. Those who witness the intifada as children might be the ones to enjoy its fruit. Yet those children are also witnessing violent and painful national liberation. They are participating in this process instead of enjoying the pleasures of carefree childhood. They too have paid a heavy price, some with their lives, and all have suffered from the extended closure of schools and other facilities. These children have been immortalized as the "children of the stones."

We spoke with Bethlehem University lecturer Dr. Jacqueline Sfeir, a specialist in early childhood education.

Editors: Our focus in this book is justice.

Jacqueline: Justice is a very relative concept. From a Palestinian perspective, what would really be justice for us as a nation is already an impossibility. It would have been just at the beginning of this conflict for it not to develop into a crisis. That would have given us as Palestinians a chance to have justice, the right to all of our land and the option to accept the Jewish nation as a component in the Palestinian state. But with the creation of the State of Israel that became impossible — not then, but now.

For possible justice to be realized, much education and action need to happen on the level of the Palestinian nation as a whole, in the Diaspora and in the Occupied Territories. We need to work out and redefine our whole future in the light of what we have now. We start off by saying, "How can we stop the clock running against us?" It is a matter of buying time. The more time passes without really addressing the issue of the Palestinian people on a human level, the more unjust any "just" solution is going to be, because all the odds are going to be against us. Just look at the intifada and what its repercussions are on the level of education, on the level of the economy, even on the level of the ecosystem and natural resources and how they are being manipulated by Israel. On all accounts justice cannot wait. The more we wait, the more we lose the option of justice.

If we are talking about justice for the Palestinian people, we must look at it from the historical point of view and must ultimately try to achieve two states, using the two states as a step toward achieving what should have already been achieved — one state with one people sharing resources. But I think that is utopia. That would be just, but so far it is not possible and not realistic to think that way. I think that in the very distant future that could happen. People will start seeing each other as people. But what we are seeing now is that the Israeli people are being brainwashed to look at the Palestinian community as monsters. They do not see us as a nation or as people. They see us as intruders, as invaders; they see us as people who threaten their existence.

These aspects have not always been present. They were not there forty years ago, when my father went to school with the Jews. My father played with Jewish neighbors, and those families did not see my father's family as a threat. They were neighbors. Now their children cannot see us as neighbors. They see us as the enemy. We see them as the enemy. Our perspectives of each other have completely changed. Not only has this occurred as a function of war, but it was a process of education. This is the hidden curriculum of education. What can you tell children about their neighbors if they feel that they cannot walk in those neighborhoods without a guard with armed protection? Those kids do not need to be told that Arabs are human, for then they would ask, "So why do I need armed protection to walk in Bethlehem or Jerusalem or anywhere that is considered an Arab neighborhood?"

These are the hidden messages taught to the children who grew up with me. Those children were the ones we encountered in the streets of Bethlehem when we were going to school. We would see flocks of schoolchildren with teachers carrying their weapons to protect them from me carrying my schoolbag going to school. I couldn't understand why those children needed protection from me. Around Christmastime why did I, as a Christian, need the protection of the army to celebrate my Christmas? Why did they have to turn Bethlehem into a military zone? They were trying to instill all these fears into us as children.

All this has to be reversed. It is not irreversible. Just as they created these realities, we have to reverse them. It is not impossible, but it takes another process to do so. If we are talking about justice, then this is the hidden agenda, the hidden curriculum. It should replace that curriculum that has created the present.

Eds.: You say that that reality was created and we can uncreate it. But realities are far more difficult to uncreate than to create. What curriculum are you suggesting to uncreate the reality?

Jacqueline: That is where you have to work on both the formal and the informal levels. The way we perceive our world is a function of the way the people around us see it. Children, who do not have preconceptions, form their value systems according to the value systems of those around them. That is why I say it is a curriculum. If the adults around those children decide to reflect a reality other than the one they have grown up with, the process of change will occur. This is why it is a very long process. Before you can get those adults to do that, you have got to work at it, and it is very difficult, but eventually it will happen. This is why I said that for us the only just peace is to start as two states to preserve that nationality, that identity, that entity, and then work together for an assimilation at a much later stage. That is not within our lifetime or that of the next few generations. To undo what has been done for half a century will need that much undoing throughout the coming centuries. In those parts of the world where there is no national conflict like we have here, the orientation is toward globalism, a world without frontiers. But you cannot go in this direction if you feel your survival is being threatened.

To relax and feel that we can re-educate our children, Israel has to stop being paranoid about everything, and the Palestinians have to come to terms with their own history and start looking at the future through new eyes. That is what we will have to start doing, respectively. Our curriculum will be to start taking the Israeli reality into consideration, and the Israeli reality has to take us into consideration. As we go along, generations will grow up that accept each other. That is the only way to a peace that is just.

Eds.: Can you tell us about some of the work you are doing as an educator?

Jacqueline: I am working with young children as an early childhood educator. I work on the level of the adult and on the level of the child separately. First, I try to present children with many options to discover themselves, their potentials and abilities, and try to help them formulate, to the utmost possibility, their own perception of the world. With the adults I try, as much as possible, to stop them from painting that picture for the children. I try to help adults get out of the way. I try to show that what is happening here is valuable in itself. I do not need my children to know everything right now; they will come to know it. I just need to trust that they will know it. My role is to be there, to be supportive and a catalyst but not a guide. I try to point out to the adults that the responsibility is not to direct but rather to keep all possibilities open and refrain from directing. The role should be to protect when protection is needed, reinforce when reinforcement is needed, and allow for whatever product that will be. It is not your choice and not your right — you do not own your children; your children are beings in their own right.

The curriculum I work with is called the process-oriented curriculum, meaning you let things happen and you have no control over the product. You create an environment that is rich with situations, and then you let the children interact with those situations. You have got to accept whatever product comes out of that situation. That is the hardest way to be a parent because the guilt that comes with the responsibility of parenthood is the disease of humankind. Parents think that it is their duty and responsibility to give their children all the options. They see the world today, and they do not have a clue how the world is going to be in twenty years when their kid is going to be an adult. So by gearing those children into a definite future that would be superb for today, twenty years later when the children are adults, all you have done is reduced the options by limiting them through defining what the best is that these kids could have now. So you are doing what you think is the best, but actually you have done the worst. You have deprived these kids of the options.

Eds.: How has the intifada affected your work?

Jacqueline: It has reinforced it both theoretically and practically. Now I feel that the teachers and the parents are much more amenable to accept the openness I suggest. They are living the uncertainty of today. Can you tell me in ten years what your kids could have as an option? You cannot even tell me about tomorrow. You want them to be doctors? But look at the doctors. You want them to be lawyers? But look at the lawyers around here. So what can they be? You do not know. So let them be. It is easier to get this across to people who have lived a struggle in any level, whether personal, political, economic, or social. It is very hard to get across to people who are settled, who feel they are the criteria, that everything is defined by their book, so you had better not tell them how their kids should be because they are going to be just like they are. That is the difficulty we face.

Thank God, 80 percent of our population is in limbo, so we do have great hope. Being a reborn state, we have so many things still to decide. There is so little decided at this point. The state is still in the making, and we are the people who are going to build the state. We have control over what that state may look like. We do have our history and culture, but concerning building the systems of the legislature, education, and all the others, we have so much to do. We have such an advantage because we have so many models to choose from.

Eds.: Some people look at the same situation and despair. They say that the children are out of control.

Jacqueline: But that is wonderful. I can understand the response because the majority does not see what I see. Resisting change is something very human. I face that in my professional life. In one place where I worked I set up a kindergarten that was an open-learning center, a big hall full of toys, without tables and chairs where the teacher could be in control. Two months later the kids loved it, and they cried when you tried to take them home. The teachers, though, resigned *en masse*. They declared that they would have nothing to do with this: "We will not take a salary and just watch the kids play. This is not why we are teachers: we are teachers to teach."

I learned a lot from that experience. I did not expect that to happen and thought I could train them. This experience happened in the microsystem. The children were not going through a revolution. They were just practicing their independence. The teachers could not take it. When you walked into the classroom, there was the humming of a busy beehive, but nothing like chaos. Teachers challenged me saying: "Within two weeks nothing will be left on the shelves. Your system is too open." I replied, "Come back in two years time, and except for the wear and tear, everything will be there." The teachers could not take it; children were behaving, and what were they supposed to do? That is what we are now experiencing on the macro-level. Children are taking over, and we do not know what to do with it. We are supposed to be the ones in charge. This is madness, but only to the ones who cannot see. We are in a good state.

Eds.: So the new person is already emerging?

Jacqueline: Oh, definitely. You see that in their drawings. Children do not understand political conflict. They do not understand history. They have trouble figuring out what yesterday was. They project through their drawings what they are trying to understand, what they are trying to formulate. They are trying to imprint their understanding of reality right now. When you see those drawings, you see that the children are most aware of their identity. You see the Palestinian flag and its colors all over the place. Those kids are definitely Palestinian. Teach them whatever you want, they are Palestinians. It is in their blood, and that is number one. Number two is the will to live. The determination to live and fight for their life is strong in kids who may be so protected that they are not allowed to go down a flight of stairs on their own, because their parents are afraid they are going to get hurt. But those kids in their hearts are ready to give everything to live that independence.

I can talk about drawings forever, but I will choose two to illustrate what I am saying. One drawing by a six-year-old child is called "The Flower of Freedom." The drawing is brown in the foreground and has little stick figures planted in the ground. The stick figures are green, depicting human beings, and their little feet are just like roots, deep down in the soil. Then the little heads start growing as you go along. It is a human chain, and the figures are holding each other's hands. Their body is confused with the flag. Each child is carrying a flag that is given to the other; it's another flag chain. From the middle of this human chain grows a flower, like a tulip; each petal has one color of the flag. This six-year-old is telling it all. It could be the declaration of independence.

Another drawing depicts a street confrontation (which is a common theme, represented in about 90 percent of the drawings I have seen) and includes the army, the shabab, the demonstration, stone throwing, bleeding Palestinians, children lying on the ground in their blood, and in the background a huge dove in the form of the Palestinian flag. In the background you can also see flowers in green, red and all kinds of colors, and the people, and their clothes are also colorful. Not a depressed child at all, but a child who depicts reality. He depicts it with this most aggressive scene, but he represents the symbol that tells us: "I know why this is happening. I know why I am putting my life on the line. I know that I am paying a price for freedom, for nationality." The drawings are all by children, and that is where truth and any value lie. It's all about them, about their future, their reality.

PART 4

RELIGIOUS PERSPECTIVES

Sheikh Akrimeh Sabri

The Occupation has taken measures to curtail religious freedom in the Occupied Territories. Thousands of Muslims have been prevented from reaching mosques to perform their prayers. In particular, harassment has been evident in the Old City of Jerusalem, which contains the third-holiest shrine in Islam: the sanctuary of the Dome of the Rock and the al-Aqsa Mosque. Palestinians have been outraged at the desecration of mosques by soldiers and their lack of respect for Islamic sensibilities. Muslim clerics have added their voice to the struggle against Occupation, often using the mosque minaret to warn people of danger or comfort people in mourning.

We spoke with Sheikh Akrimeh Sabri, a member of the Supreme Muslim Council and an Islamic correspondent of the Palestinian daily newspaper *al-Quds*.

Editors: How do you think the intifada has focused issues of justice in the Palestinian community?

Akrimeh: It is a known fact that whenever injustice is imposed on people, they will attempt to remove this injustice, in any way that they see fit and according to the possibilities available to them. Thereafter they will demand justice to achieve their rights. Who knows better the value of justice than those who suffer injustice? When the Palestinian people began their intifada, they were experiencing enormous injustice. Therefore they demanded justice — the establishment of a Palestinian state on their national soil. The intifada caused the entire world, both inside and outside the Middle East, to realize that the Palestinian people are suffering injustice.

I have written a number of articles and lectured frequently on the subject of justice and right. It cannot be that justice and right are always on the side of the strong. Of course, they also cannot always be with the weak. The strong should not always exploit their power to impose their will on the weak by issuing laws and statutes to serve their own special interests. At the same time, such laws oppress the weak. This only perpetrates injustice. Justice is realized through mutual respect and honoring the rights of others.

Eds.: How would you formulate a just solution to the particular struggle here between Palestinians and Israelis?

Akrimeh: Justice necessarily precedes peace. Peace is inconceivable without justice. This land is the Land of Palestine, a blessed land. No one can deny that people of the three heavenly religions have a right here and are connected with this land. Therefore no one side can claim that the land is its exclusively. The Muslims ruled this land for thirteen centuries, and then it was taken from them by force. It is said and repeated that Transjordan is the home of the Palestinians, but this is completely absurd and unacceptable. There is no other way but for the Palestinians to be granted their own independent state, and for there to be a kind of mutual respect, a recognition of the rights of all sides. The presence of those living here now is threatened by the arrival of new immigrants. We must not forget the need for the realization of justice and a solution, but this type of immigration is a type of unnecessary complication.

Eds.: What is the role of Islam in all this?

Akrimeh: We must stress that Islam is not against the other religions. This is the first point. Second, Islam calls for justice for both Muslims and non-Muslims. Third, the fact that the Muslims are returning to their religion does not mean that they are terrorists and murderers. Fourth, Islam does not prevent those of other religions from holding onto their religions. Every group can practice its religion. In fact, when Muslims feel that Christians are practicing their religion and Jews are practicing their religion, they realize that this brings them closer together and does not distance them. Islam is not a dangerous phenomenon and should not be perceived as being against other nations. The big powers, like America and Britain, possibly sense that

Islam is a dangerous phenomenon because Islam seeks to weaken their influence on this land.

The intifada itself does not have a specific religious direction. Rather, the entire people have taken stock of the injustice and have begun to shake it off. This was a result of the injustice. It was obvious that this Occupation practiced cruel treatment against this people. They turned to God and to religion. The Palestinian leadership warned the world concerning any delay in finding a peaceful solution. Time is not on the side of the great powers. When is the ruling force, it will not accept these rather weak and lean peace efforts.

Everyone works against the Occupation. Whether part of the Unified Leadership or HAMAS or ordinary citizens, all hate it and resent it and see themselves as the nucleus of the intifada. The issue is not one of individuals or of certain leaders. They can arrest tens of thousands, and yet each of those left will see themselves as responsible.

The thing that most influences the youth is the torture in the prisons and the methods of interrogation. The Jews themselves have suffered under Nazism and Fascism and torture. How can these people now torture others? This is a mistake. If I had suffered injustice in the past, I should be sensitive to the one suffering injustice now. I should not use the same methods. In all the prisons there is very cruel torture. So now what is the difference between this and Hitler? You say you do not want Hitler and you do not want Nazism, so why are you murdering now? Shame on you! Thousands of youth in the West Bank and Gaza Strip are crippled because they were beaten on the spine, or they have suffered cerebral concussion from being beaten on the head. Some have lost their eyes or their hearing. Some have had arms and legs amputated. There are more than ten thousand of these cripples. This does not even include those who have died under the stick. These are Fascist methods, and the families are going to revolt even more; they are not going to give in as a result but rather will increase their opposition.

A verse from a poem says, "Act well with people, and through that, you will subdue their hearts." Kindness makes the person your slave. This means that if you act well toward another, you will be able to penetrate that person's heart. People will love you through your good treatment of them. But on this basis it cannot be expected that the Palestinian people would like the present authorities. They know nothing of this goodness but rather only know how these authorities confiscate lands, restrict people to their homes, detain and deport. Is it any wonder, then, that they are hated?

This separation between Jews and Arabs is a direct result of the authorities. Last week I read in the newspapers about the burning of the Burin Mosque, in the area of Nablus. Why was this done? This is a mosque, a house of God for worship. If a synagogue was burned, what would the Jews do? They would overturn heaven and earth. Yet this is a mosque, and in it there were holy books, texts of the Qur'an. I saw this all with my own eyes because I went there. In Hebron I saw texts of the Holy Qur'an scribbled over and desecrated. The Star of David and curses about our Prophet Muhammad, peace be upon him, were drawn over the Holy Qur'an. Why does this happen? What good can possibly come from it? Do you think Muslims will simply remain Muslims as before, or will they rather increase their devotion to religion? We as Muslims are directed by the Holy Qur'an to preserve the feelings and rituals of the other heavenly religions. This is fundamental, and it is an obligation. These activities that are directed at the sensitivities of Muslims only increase support for HAMAS. It is as if through these acts the soldiers and the settlers were saying to the Muslims, "Go join HAMAS!"

Eds.: The authorities have tried to separate Muslims and Christians. How has the intifada affected the relationship?

Akrimeh: There is no doubt that the intifada has created a national unity of the people. Although one sees that Muslims are saying that Muslims must be more devoted to their religion, one can see that they say the same thing to Christians in Bethlehem, Bayt Sahur, Bayt Jalla, and Ramallah: Be more devoted to your religion. The intifada has undoubtedly drawn Muslims and Christians closer together. There are clear attempts to divide. This is clear in the media, but the people are fully conscious and understand. It is not possible that the authorities will succeed in dividing Muslims and Christians.

Father George Makhlouf

Although Palestinian Christians are a tiny minority in the Occupied Territories, their role in the intifada has been a prominent one. Heads of the Christian churches — Greek Orthodox, Roman Catholic, Armenian, Greek Catholic, Anglican, and others — have repeatedly condemned the violations of human rights. Since the beginning of the intifada all the Christian celebrations of Easter and Christmas and other feasts have been severely curtailed as a sign of respect for those who have given their lives in the struggle against Occupation, including a number of Christian Palestinian youths. Predominantly Christian Palestinian towns have been at the forefront of the intifada, joining with their Muslim Palestinian neighbors.

We spoke with Father George Makhlouf, Greek Orthodox priest of the town of Ramallah on the West Bank.

Editors: How has the intifada clarified the concept of justice in the Israeli-Palestinian struggle?

George: I think that the intifada has gone beyond justice. It is over forty years since the displacement of the Palestinian people, and now it is too late to talk about justice. If we want to stress justice concerning the Palestinian problem, justice has only one meaning — UN Resolution 194, which is the Right of Return for the Palestinian people.

But I see the intifada as a peace process, because the Palestinians gave up their traditional just claims. In Algiers on November 15, 1988, the PNC, which is the Palestinian parliament, made very generous concessions for the sake of peace. Palestinians have rejected violence. Palestinians recognize now the right of self-determination for the Jews. We realize that Israel has the right to exist, and we agree to this, even though we have made a great sacrifice in this by relinquishing our grandparents' homes. The Algiers conference was a kind of "waiver and relinquish" for the sake of peace.

The intifada undoubtedly clarifies some issues of justice: that all human beings are equal in rights and in duties, that there must not be a ruler people and a ruled people, that the act of transfer is illegal, that there should be no taxation without representation, that representatives of the Palestinian people should not be nominated by their enemies. We Palestinians are milked dry by the Occupation, which imposes crippling taxes, raking in additional funds from fining us, arresting our children, and setting extravagant bail. We have never seen any fruit from this money, and the services offered in return for the taxes are absolutely minimal. Refusal to pay taxes, which are spent on keeping us under Occupation, has been a prominent feature of the intifada. These are some of the issues that the intifada has clarified.

My role in my community as a religious person is to teach people how to forgive. Our Lord forgave his crucifiers, and so I keep telling my parishioners that we do not forgive those who did not trespass against us but forgive those who did wrong. This is our preparation for our future.

I have been a victim myself. I was born in West Jerusalem. At about the age of five, I was displaced. My mother finally convinced my father that the time had come for us to leave and find a safer place. There had been artillery clashes, and many people were killed in the surrounding area. There were incidents like the destruction of the King David Hotel and the killing of Count Bernadotte. My mother was very afraid because of terrorist actions, and, like every mother, she wanted safety for her children. We went to a village where the Jews could not reach us. We had before our eyes what had happened in Deir Yassin and the many other massacres that took place.

But we should not focus on the past. The most important thing now for a Christian, and in fact for any Arab, is to learn how to forgive others. I remember a story of the great Muslim ruler Umar bin Khattab, who had an opponent. Umar would sleep in the desert. One day he found a sword in the sand next to him. This was a sign that stated, I could have killed you, but I did not — the signature of forgiveness. This is our tradition and a part of our culture. We have to forgive, yet you don't forgive your friend, those who cause no hurt or harm, but rather those who hurt you.

I was raised in East Jerusalem. All the beautiful things — the front yard, the back yard, the Christmas tree, the toys — that remind one of childhood were at a stone's throw from where I was. For nineteen years I felt jealous of the cats, dogs, and pigeons. They could cross the fence from one side to the other, but I could not. I was deeply hurt. When the 1967 war was waged and the small part of Palestine that remained was also occupied, it was an opportunity for me to visit the house where I was born. I was very badly treated over there — beaten and kicked out of my house.

When you feel that you have been dealt with unjustly, you start to appreciate the value of justice. When the electricity is cut, then you appreciate light; when you are lost in the desert, then you appreciate water. Thus as we have been unjustly dealt with in so many ways, and still every day are continuously being dealt with unjustly, we know the value of justice. We also are heirs to the religious concept "Do unto others as you want them to do unto you," which is my rule to preach. We cannot separate peace from justice. We feel that peace is a right.

Eds.: When you give a sermon in church, how do you deal with the themes of love, peace, forgiveness, and justice?

George: Everybody says that it is hard to be a good Christian, not only in Palestine, but throughout the world. In church we tell them that we fight with oppression, not with the oppressors; with discrimination, not with the racist; with injustice, not with the unjust. We practice our right of resistance, which is a peaceful resistance. I do not pay tax. I refuse to be exploited financially. I refuse to bribe in order to get through a formality. This is a right, and it is a peaceful way of resistance. You have the right to resist, and this is Christian teaching too. Gandhi was not a Christian, but his form of resistance is a model. Jesus Christ himself resisted. He said to the man who slapped him: "Oh, my friend, what wrong have I done you? I have done nothing wrong." He raised his voice, and when we raise our voices in resistance, we imitate Jesus Christ. Jesus Christ went to the temple and overthrew the tables of the money-changers. He proclaimed that his Father's house was a place for prayer, not for thieving merchants and robbers.

We who are under Occupation have the right of resistance. Our leadership in Tunisia said that the resistance should be peaceful resistance without weapons. This is a pure Christian approach. But to what extent would the people psychologically be able to restrain themselves? We teach love and nonviolence, but if you pump gas into a confined container, then the explosion, whether you like it or not, will be enormous. Some are calling for violence, but these are at present voices from the outside, and our Palestinian leadership says no to them. But people ask: "Till when? How long?"

Eds.: Zionism has tried to interpret the religious tradition as teaching that the land has been given to the Jews. Many Christian Zionists have accepted this logic.

George: I am glad that you raise this point. All that we hear is very new. The teaching of the Fathers, the teaching of the Bible, the teaching of Christian tradition and theology in no way support this heresy. You know that Judaism is the old leaven. Jesus Christ came to those who belonged to him, but they refused him, so he elected the Gentile church. New Zion is the Church of the Gentiles. Israel is the Church of Jerusalem. These people, who have been here since time immemorial, are the grandchildren of the Apostles and of the Patriarchs — Abraham, Isaac, and Jacob.

Aside from all this, we need to examine what the term "Promised Land" means. God is not dead or dying, and therefore God does not leave a certain people an inheritance. The promises of God are eternal but are of a spiritual and not a material nature. We have always understood "Promised Land" to mean Jesus Christ, who comes to dwell within us.

God intervenes in everything; God has a finger in history and in everyday action. We cannot say that theology does not deal with everyday life. I am a Christian not only when I worship but at every moment — when I am asleep, when I am awake, when I eat, when I work. Therefore the old preachers who would say that there is no homeland for us here on earth, that our true homeland is in heaven, were wrong. Jesus Christ came to redeem you and me and everybody as we are. He wants to redeem me as a Palestinian. From 1948 until 1987 religious preachers taught that Christian believers have no lasting city on this earth, that their nation is in heaven. But the intifada has awakened the minds of Palestinian theologians, and they have started to see that the acts of God, God's intervention in everyday life, are a fact.

When I see a martyr, I cannot but think of the words of Christ, "No greater love have they than those who give their life for those they love." When I see these children throwing rocks, I remember David and Goliath. I remember that Jesus himself was the cornerstone that was rejected by the builders; I remember that he told the disciples, "If these children fall silent, then the stones themselves will shout out." Now we see that the time has come when God has indeed made the stones speak. God is a God of peace and justice. God is a universal God, not the God of one nation. God is a God of love, not a God of discrimination and racism. We believe in a God of peace and not in a belligerent God.

We find now that ecumenism has become a living reality throughout the Christian communities of Jerusalem and the Holy Land. Religious leaders have signed statements together in the name of justice. Christian leaders were expelled together from the village of Bayt Sahur, prevented from attending to the needs of their sheep. They had this experience together, of a father who could not reach his son. They had gone because of their religious and human duty to console their children. Is there no freedom? The intifada has clarified the right to freedom of worship and the right of religious thinking. This is just and fair.

When I go to Nativity Church on Christmas, I am confronted there, despite myself, with Shaike Erez [the Israeli military governor], whose hands are full of Palestinian blood. This provokes me while I am worshipping God and praying for peace. His presence there distracts me from keeping my eyes fixed on God to praise and worship God. Perhaps his presence tells me that I must forgive my enemies, but it is difficult when you see policemen inside the church laughing and making fun of the ceremony, see Israeli children misbehave, expressing their affections for one another inside the church, the very church where the Holy Virgin gave birth to the Son in purity and chastity. When I go to celebrate my liturgy as a cleric, I have to purify myself; I have to abstain from sexual contact and fast. Nowhere else in the world do people going to worship have to pass through security checks. Only Palestinians, when they go and worship, have to be inspected, because Shaike Erez wants to come and participate in the ceremony. Well, who sent for him? He is not supposed to be there.

Cooperation between Muslims and Christians is a very old phenomenon in the history of this land. Unfortunately America has supported the so-called fundamentalists, pushing forward religious fanaticism, believing that this will limit the expansion of Communism. This is another harmful thing that has come to us from the United States. Remember that in the twelfth century Muslims and Christians stood together to fight the oppressors, the Crusaders, who came from the West to colonize our homeland. They came to Palestine after having passed through Constantinople, where they destroyed the Orthodox Byzantine churches and stole the skull of St. Andrew, the relics of St. Sabba from Palestine, and so forth. But here, under Saladin, Muslims and Christians fought together against foreign oppressors. There is a degree of fanaticism among the Muslims, but this is fed by the Western colonialists, who want to split up the one united people.

Eds.: How do you see a just solution to the conflict?

George: I think that the concessions offered by the Palestinians, including their acceptance of the right of Israel to exist and acceptance of Lord Caredon's Resolution 242, prepare the way for a solution. I think that Resolution 242 must be applied to the full. As we recognize their right of self-determination, so must they recognize our right of self-determination — not in Transjordan but in our grandparents' land. We do not want Transjordan. The unity between Palestine and Transjordan was a bad experience, and we do not want it anymore. Resolution 181 states that there must be two countries for two peoples. There might be a federal unity between them. Why not? But not with Transjordan. We are not Arab nationalists but rather Palestinian nationalists. They want to consider all the Middle East peoples as undifferentiated Arabs. We say no: We are Palestinians. As Palestinians, we demand our self-determination. We have to find a place for the refugees who are suffering in the camps before we bring here more Diaspora Jews. I think that the Algiers resolution of November 1988 is the solution. This is the Palestinian peace. This is justice for us as Palestinians. We cannot make any more concessions.

Dr. Yisrael Eldad

The intifada has led to an extreme polarization of Israeli political life. Those calling for a two-states solution have faced strong opposition from a vigorous right wing, which promotes the idea of a Greater Israel and the annexation of the Occupied Territories. This right wing has insisted that "the Palestinian problem" is the creation of a hostile Arab world that refuses to recognize the State of Israel. In the opinion of the right wing, Jewish history, especially in Europe, has shown that Israel must stand firm against all pressure if it is to preserve Jewish communal life.

We spoke with Dr. Yisrael Eldad, a noted publicist and educator and one of the grand old men of the Israeli right wing.

Editors: How can we reach a just solution to the Palestinian-Israeli conflict?

Yisrael: First, concepts like "just" and "justice" should be properly situated within their correct context — but they actually have no proper context. All people perceive their own justice, and I have almost never heard an objective definition. To "do justice," one has to be master of the world, and even then I am not so sure that there is justice. Read the Book of Job. If doubts are cast even on the justice of the Creator of the world, what can be expected from flesh and blood fighting to survive? When we discuss justice, we must examine who is asking about it and who is responding. When I lecture about history and Zionism, the first thing I declare is that I am subjective. If people say that they are objective, do not believe them. I am subjective because I am a Jew; I am a Zionist, and I speak from a particular perspective. But the moment I announce that I am in fact subjective and then inform you from which perspective I am speaking, then what I am saying takes on an objective character.

I do not want to speak about absolute justice because I do not know what it is. I am also not interested in it because I am flesh and blood. I am interested in my perspective and that of my grandchildren, and not in absolute justice. Thus I have presented the claimant, the one arguing for justice. Now no one will expect me to address the issue of justice from the perspective of the Palestinians. This is not my concern.

In the medieval period the church argued that Israel had completed its vocation and had no future. The church was the inheritor of the spiritual gifts, although there was always a dispute within the church whether this inheritance included the land and Jerusalem or not. There was only one problem with the claim: one can inherit only from someone who has died. The People of Israel, to the great disappointment of many, have not died. If the people have not died, then you cannot take these things from them. The land is therefore theirs because of the promise. Christians accept the Bible and the promise. What do you do if not only is Israel alive, but it also has a call to this same land, based upon the promise, which you recognize as authentic through the Bible and prophecy? Here we are; we have been resurrected, and we are no longer waiting for a Messiah to come but want to be our own redeemers. We proclaim that you cannot take the inheritance from the living, nor can you give it to others.

Many Christians identify with the Palestinians and want to give them the land. I cannot demand anything from the Chinese, but Christians — whether Evangelicals, Catholics, or Protestants, all of them basing themselves upon the Hebrew Bible and prophecy — know to whom God promised this land. How can they possibly have the nerve to come and demand the land from us and give it wholly or partially to the Palestinians?

I am not speaking politics here; politics is another matter, and there pragmatic issues, like oil, determine decisions. That is legitimate. But here we are addressing Christians in the name of their faith, and in this area, justice — divine justice, religious justice, and the promise — should play a part, not oil. Therefore, as concerns justice, the Christian world is obligated not only to support the Jewish claim but to do much more. After two thousand years they have learned that the Jews do not want to leave their faith and their religion. Only on the basis of this recognition can any cooperation or understanding be reached. This was to some extent behind the Balfour Declaration. Lloyd George argued that aside from all the imperialist interests, he would not deny that his religious education, based on the Old Testament, had been a major motivation for the declaration. I demand that Christians take a stand alongside us.

If justice really did prevail in Christianity and in the Christian churches, then not only would they have given the Balfour Declaration but, after the Holocaust, when the pope visited the land for the first time, he would have come here on his knees to the Jewish people in Jerusalem to beg their forgiveness. If it had not been for all those pogroms, the Crusades, the Black Death, and the massacres, we would be a people numbering ninety million today. Sociologists have estimated this. Christians should come on their knees and beg forgiveness and in the name of justice support us here in our claims.

Eds.: Some Christians do warmly support Israel, yet among these supporters are the biggest anti-Semites, those who see Zionism as a way to get rid of the Jews by creating a ghetto in Israel. And there are churches who want to exorcize anti-Semitism but who do not see why the Palestinians should suffer for the sins of Christians.

Yisrael: I do not care whether these churches are Zionist or not. There are few enough Jews who are really Zionist. Zionism was not established for Zionists. Some say that the Jews coming now from Russia are not Zionists. But this is a classic Zionist immigration. Herzl created Zionism for Jews in crisis, not for Zionists. Abraham, our father, was a Zionist. God told him, "Go forth," and he got up and went. Even in leaving Egypt, the Jews were not Zionists; they were escaping from crisis. It is impossible to demand that a whole people be idealists; after all, Moses was alone when he ascended Mount Sinai. The people were left at the foot of the mountain. The people are always down there, and the law had to be imposed on this people. The miracle is that there are those few idealists.

Since the days of Herzl, Zionists have been accused of being allied with anti-Semites. This is true, though we must clarify what we mean by "ally." There are objective and subjective allies. When a person is sick, the fever is the ally of the doctor. Sores on the body are the ally of the doctor. The situation of the Jews is that the Diaspora is a disease, an abnormal situation. Napoleon understood, and he was the first one to offer the Land of Israel to the Jews in modern times. When he was on Mount Tabor, passing through the land, he sat down with a French rabbi and addressed a call to the Jews. This was in 1798 or 1799. But there was no address for the Jewish people then. In the days of the Balfour Declaration there was already an address. This is the most important thing contributed by Zionism: Herzl gave the Jewish people an address.

The slavery in Egypt was an ally of Zionism, like the microbes being the allies of the doctor. When we give antibiotics, there is mold inside them. Within this mold there are germs — that is, disease — but they are essential for the cure. This is anti-Semitism.

Anti-Semitism serves as a reminder both to us and to the non-Jews. Fichte, one of Kant's brightest students, wrote, during the blossoming of the Jewish Emancipation: "We must finish the Jews off. If we could lop off their heads and give them other heads, it would be good. But because we cannot, the best thing we can do is to conquer the Holy Land and send all the Jews there." This is a typical anti-Semitic Zionist. I believe in Zionism, and I want the Jews to live here by any means.

Wherever it is good for the Jews, they tend to assimilate. Trouble for the Jews is the price for saving the people and its existence.

And now, what about the Palestinians in all this? Until now I have been speaking about justice as it relates to my conflict with Christianity. But now you say that there are Palestinians here. Of course the Arab response to this whole argument is, Jewish crisis? Fine, but why at our expense? This is logical. But on closer examination this is not just at all; justice is solely ours. Look, they tried to offer us Uganda, Birobidzhan, and many other places, but we did not take them because we wanted to come home. Ben-Gurion once said that whoever does not believe in miracles in the Land of Israel is not a realist. The present immigration from Russia is one of those miracles in history. They are not Zionists; they simply say, "We have come home." The Arabs are quite right to oppose this immigration. It is not a problem of territories or anything else. Their campaign, from their point of view, is indeed just. The return is to the Land of Israel, never mind the temporary borders of any political agreement. Ben-Gurion recognized this when he agreed to partition, but he did not see this as permanent partition.

The return is not just to some territory. There was a territorial Zionist movement, but if the matter is just territory, then why not Uganda? Because it is not a matter of territory at all. The push created by the crisis of Jews wherever they might be is only an additional motivation. It inflames the already-existing motivation. For two thousand years they prayed for a Messiah and a return to Zion. Look, we have returned and revived Hebrew as our language.

The whole matter of return is not just a matter of crisis of Jews or of territory. If you are in crisis, go to America. So what about the Palestinians? We are returning home! The whole world should understand this, that we are returning home, not just coming here out of the blue. I often lecture about Jerusalem, and I do not like the phrase "sacred to three religions." It is not that Jerusalem is not holy for Christians and Muslims; I cannot determine this for them. I oppose this talk, though, of a supposed common factor. There is no common factor in its holiness to us and its holiness to Christians and Muslims. For Christians, the belief is that here Jesus was crucified and here he was resurrected. For Muslims, the belief is connected to some dream of Muhammad, that Gabriel took him up into heaven from the Temple Mount. Is our claim based on anything miraculous? King David conquered the city, and he even bought the Temple Mount. He fixed here the geopolitical and strategic priorities of his kingdom. This was the capital of the

Jewish people. Because of its being the capital of the Jewish people, there are miracles associated with it, but its centrality for Jews is not because of these miracles.

For Christians and Muslims, the land is holy because of some incidents and not because of history. For us, Jerusalem is holy because of history. We have created things here that we have given to the whole world. Since we left this land nothing spiritual was created here, nothing of any value. I do not know of one worthwhile book, whether from the Byzantine, Muslim, Crusader, or Turkish period. The land produced nothing. The land blossomed under the Byzantines, and the Crusaders left behind some architectural edifices, but nothing spiritual. There was never a Palestinian Arab state here. The whole concept of a Palestinian people is counterfeit. We have lived here and created here; we were exiled from the land, but we remained spiritually faithful to it through the centuries. We never forgot it. We did not say to ourselves, "Come, let us go and conquer a land for ourselves!" We have not created a new national identity. We did not rule the Land of Israel for two thousand years, but no other political entity appeared here in the interim.

We did not take the state from the Palestinians, so how can they argue, "You invaded us, and now give it back"? The Russians invaded Afghanistan, and they should get out. The Russians invaded Lithuania, and they should get out. But we did not invade a state; we did not destroy a state; they did not come home as we did. In addition, it is most probable that Russia can live without Lithuania. Likewise it is possible that the people that calls itself Palestinian can live without the Land of Israel because they have twenty-two other Arab countries. The Arabs of the Land of Israel are a part of the greater Arab world.

Eds.: Would you say that this is a just solution, that the Arabs who live here should find their identity within the framework of those twenty-two Arab states?

Yisrael: But they do not have any sense of identity. They have no history. Who knows the history of the Palestinians? Until twenty years ago, they had no literature. Look, nationalism has to have some signs. If they do want to claim nationhood, then why here? This is not an empty space. I can point out alternatives for them, but I cannot think of any alternatives for us. We have the promise from God, we have the history of a presence here, we have a Holocaust, which no Arab people can say they anticipate. If the problem is natives, then where are we supposed to go? To the North Pole? In every area there are natives. If I am always faced by this reality of natives, then I will go to the place where there is a historical justification.

I do not say that there could never be a Palestinian nation. It is true that tribes pick themselves up and proclaim themselves nations without any basis in reality. But to that I also have an answer. Justice versus justice. Then I bring all my claims — historical, religious, the Holocaust, and so forth. But most importantly, the Jewish people have already conceded two-thirds of their homeland. In the Balfour Declaration and in the international mandate, the Land of Israel consisted of two banks of the Jordan River. Let us not even talk about the land between the Euphrates and the Nile, which was the promise to Abraham our father. Britain committed itself to two banks of the Jordan River.

Now Jordan is even less of a nation than Palestine. What is Jordan? What are the people of Jordan? This country arose through the manipulations of Lawrence of Arabia and Churchill. They did not know what to do with Abdullah, who was wandering around with his five hundred camel drivers on his way to help Faysal in Damascus and got stuck in the middle. Faysal was given Iraq, and Abdullah was given Jordan out of ultra-imperialist motives. This Jordanian state is a complete vanity of vanities. Today the reality is that 70 percent of the Jordanian population is Palestinian. If Jordan were a democracy, it would have become a Palestinian state, and Hussein knows that. I, the "extremist," the "pseudo-Fascist," the "imperialist Zionist," who was raised on Jabotinsky's anthem "Two banks has the Jordan River; this one is ours, and so is that one" — I am prepared to renounce my right to that bank. This is the solution. Let them establish a democracy there, where they already are 70 percent. Let them call it Palestine or whatever they want.

Now what about the intifada? For us it is a very bad thing because it certainly strengthens the Palestinian sense of identity. I, as a graduate of LEHI — Freedom Fighters of Israel, a pre-1948 underground militia — respect this will to fight for the land. The blood that is shed works. But I must say that even LEHI, which was the most fanatic of the pre-1948 underground militias, directed its war solely against British soldiers; we never killed women or children. We could have blown up British schools full of children quite easily, as they were not under guard. Yitzhaq Shamir and I were central planners of military operations, but it never entered our minds to blow up a school or a school bus. But they even do this to one another.

Look at Lebanon, where it is even Christian against Christian. What is going on there? It is no longer a question of Christian against Muslim, Syria against Lebanon, but Christians among themselves. Where is the world? Where is the hypocritical Christian world? The world makes a big noise about the two or three Arabs who are killed every day here, but what about what is going on there, with five hundred dead in a few days? Where is the pope? Why is he suddenly silent? They do not honor the agreements among themselves, things signed between one Lebanese Christian and another. How can we expect, then, that Arafat or any of them will honor an agreement signed with us?

So what should be done now? Transjordan is a solution to the Palestinian refugee problem. This problem is very acute. For forty years this problem has remained unsolved. Over the years the refugee problem in other parts of the world has been solved. Look how forty million Germans solved the refugee problem of twelve million Germans. The Arab world is rich. Why have they not solved the problem of their brothers? We solved an enormous refugee problem of Jews from Europe and the Arab countries. In the early years we absorbed six times the number of our population.

The intifada is most severe among these refugees who have nothing to lose and who live in very difficult conditions. Some Jews cry over the refugee camps and want to give away only Judea and Samaria. Are they prepared to give away Ramat Aviv, built on Arab land, or the Hebrew University, built on Arab land? The refugees are largely from inside the 1948 borders: they have already been uprooted, so what is the difference, in humanitarian terms, if you resettle them twenty kilometers from their home or sixty kilometers from their home?

From the military point of view, I am for collective punishment. Soldiers chasing after children turn a political problem into a police problem. They catch the boy who threw the stone and they put him on trial, but this is not a problem of criminal activity. We graduates of LEHI understand that this is a political matter. They are fighting a political war. I do not want to chase them as if they were criminals. He is my political enemy. I should treat him as such. If a Palestinian village or a university riots, then we should gather the villagers or all the students and professors and simply transfer them to Transjordan. This should be without violence; I cannot stand seeing the soldiers beating civilians. Anyway, beating does not deter them, neither will death sentences. They are patriots, believing in martyrdom for the cause. This is a war, and they see it as a war. If they feel that they are succeeding, then there is no reason why the Arabs in Galilee could not tomorrow initiate their own intifada. Today they are already more than 50 percent. It is a natural irredentist movement.

I once had a debate with the late Abd al-Aziz Zu'bi, [an Arab] deputy minister of health [in Israel]. I said to him: "We have been praying for two thousand years in the direction of Jerusalem, and at last we have arrived. Where do you pray to? Mecca. I hope you too arrive."

Rev. Shehade Shehade

Israel/Palestine has not always witnessed violent conflict among the religious communities that have invested so much significance in the Holy Land. Jews, who see Jerusalem as the center of the religious world, Christians, who see Jerusalem as the backdrop to the crucifixion and resurrection of Christ, and Muslims, who see Jerusalem as the first direction of prayer and the third sanctuary, have lived side by side for centuries. Although religion has often been mobilized by the national movements of the two parties of the conflict, the intifada has also seen the rebirth of prophetic religion calling for justice and peace.

We spoke with Reverend Shehade Shehade, Anglican minister of the Galilee village of Kafr Yasif, head of the Committee for the Defence of Land and a founder of Clergy for Peace.

Shehade: I am a pastor, and this is the first thing that moved me to work toward reconciliation and understanding between communities and ideologies in conflict. This is strengthened by the fact that I am an Israeli citizen, although I am a Palestinian, living in a situation that I would not wish on others. We have lived under great pressure since 1948, and this has been expressed through the discrimination we have suffered since that time. This discrimination has taken many forms: the expropriation of land, discrimination against our workers, allocating lower budgets to our Palestinian towns and villages, fewer opportunities to find work, lack of planning for our agriculture, and no irrigation systems for our farmers. This situation motivated me, as a minister, to look at things differently, realizing that this situation cannot continue indefinitely. I believed that we should start organizing ourselves as peace lovers, people who want to live together in Palestine/Israel. I first started working through my church as a peacemaker and then through various institutions in Israel and abroad.

The main drive for setting out on this path was my Jesus. This is the Jesus who accepts suffering for the sins of the people. Discrimination is the sin of people, but that does not mean that I accept such sins as given. We must fight against this but not even with stones, although I do recognize the stones of the intifada as holy stones. We are human beings, which means we can reach a situation where societies or parties in conflict can sit together and talk with one another to remove the misunderstandings in the minds of people and the stereotypes that have been cultivated by politicians. These things are important to our work as peace lovers and peacemakers.

I see myself more as a peace fighter. A peace worker is sometimes troubled by doubts, and sometimes he or she may reach a certain point where work must be stopped because there is no more to offer, there has been a loss of hope. But the peace fighter is the one who keeps on fighting for peace until death, like Jesus on the Cross. This is what motivates me, and I work out of my Christian conviction. I am willing to work with any party, any group, or any movement that looks for peace.

Editors: As a Christian Palestinian and as a minister, what do you say to those who argue that Israel's *raison d'être* is in the Bible?

Shehade: This is one of the major theological issues that is still debated in many Christian circles. I do believe, though, that the major Christian churches have come to some understanding on this issue. There is a great difference between the present political Israel and the Israel of the Bible. Unfortunately some Christians relate to the establishment of the State of Israel as to the Second Coming of Jesus Christ. They quote verses from Isaiah, Ezekiel, and Daniel, picking verses at random, quoting out of context, and interpreting the verses according to their own understanding. Such interpretation is purely political and has no religious aim.

Does a Christian consider prophecy as something like soothsaying? Is prophecy really predicting the future two thousand or three thousand years after it was written? Or does prophecy mean, to Christians and Jews, that this Word of God speaks to a certain situation, a certain people, at a certain time? The three Isaiahs speak about the return from exile. But this is a return from exile at the time and does not say anything about a return from exile now.

As relates to the Second Coming of Christ, I have often wondered how Christians dared connect this with the establishment of the State of Israel. Some Christians believe that before the Second Coming certain awful events should take place — wars, bloodshed, killing thousands of people — all in preparation. But I ask myself, as a Christian and student of theology, is it really true that the preparation for Christ's Second Coming is through war and bloodshed? I have seen through our Bible, through the Old and New Testaments, how Jesus came the first time. He constantly rejected the idea of war and power. He taught that we must love our enemies. Is it possible that this humble figure, the Word of God who came to redeem the people from their sins, accepting suffering on the Cross to reconcile human beings with each other and with God, will come a second time through war and bloodshed, through killing and crime? This is not Christian thinking, and I reject it completely. Jesus is coming to redeem, to build his kingdom of peace and understanding and reconciliation. This is my view of Israel in the context of the Old and New Testaments.

Eds.: What political solution do you propose to the conflict?

Shehade: I believe that the two-states solution is the ideal solution, at least for the present time. Both Palestinians and Israeli Jews have a dream to build their own states. I am not talking about the ideal now, but rather about the practical implementation of a solution for permanent peace in the Middle East among Jews, Palestinians, and the Arab world at large. To fulfil a dream, you must allow for the opportunity to put it into practice. Realistically, the Jews want their own independent state, so let them have it. Palestinians want their own independent state alongside Israel, in the West Bank and Gaza Strip, so let them have it. I am sure that this is the right solution for now. I oppose talk of a secular state because I think it would create more problems. Yet a secular state for both peoples is the ideal. I am sure that in the future we are going to realize that there should be one secular state for both peoples.

People have always been told that Jews and Palestinians have been enemies since time immemorial, but this is not true. I can assure you that we Palestinians have lived alongside Jews harmoniously for centuries. Most of the time we were under foreign occupation together, but we lived through that all in peace and harmony. The problems began with the beginning of the Zionist movement in 1897, which proposed that this was "a land without a people for a people without a land." But we Palestinians have always been here, since time immemorial, as farmers who tilled the land, as workers who lived and died on the land.

Serious clashes between the two communities did not begin until after 1917, when the Balfour Declaration, made by the British, promised the land to the Jews. The British mandate, which was in power here for thirty years, helped the Jews fulfil their dream while ignoring the dreams and sensitivities of the Palestinians. Too late the British realized their mistake and offered a two-states solution — partition of the country between Jews and Palestinians. I know that the Palestinian leadership and the other Arab countries made the big mistake of saying no to the partition plan, but even if they had said yes, it would have been impossible to implement. The proposed Jewish state had 500,000 Jewish residents and 490,000 Palestinian residents. Throughout history, Palestinians have never really had the freedom to choose their own future. They lived under the Turks for more than four hundred years and then under the British mandate for thirty years. Now they are dispersed in the Arab countries and in Israel and the Occupied Territories. A few years ago the Palestinians decided to take their fate into their own hands, thanked the Arab countries for supporting their cause, and demanded the right to make their own decisions. This was an important step for Palestinians and Jews alike.

Eds.: What are you doing to promote what you believe in?

Shehade: I am a Christian Palestinian, living in Israel in a small town of six thousand people called Kafr Yasif in Galilee, in northern Israel. On observing the events of the intifada over the past two years, I realized that it was our duty as Christians to do something. I started making contact with my friends and colleagues, clergy of all faiths, Christians as well as Jews, Muslims and Druze. We began by establishing a committee to continue the work. In our discussions we decided to organize a meeting of Christians, Muslims, Druze, and Jews to express our spiritual understanding of what is happening in the West Bank and the Gaza Strip and the injustices that are committed there by the Israeli authorities. We had seventy clerics at the meeting, the first of its kind in the history of the area. It was a great success. The meeting led us to reflect on the continuation of our work for peace and reconciliation through spiritual conviction. We decided to establish an organization called Clergy for Peace, and we have Jewish, Druze, Muslim, and Christian (Greek Catholic, Greek Orthodox, and Anglican) members. We do not have an office, but we do have two coordinators — a Jew, liberal rabbi Jeremy Milgrom, and myself.

Our aim is to work for the reconciliation of Jews and Palestinians through nonpolitical means. Although we do say "nonpolitical," you cannot but deal with politics when you speak about justice, reconciliation, and the right of a people to recognition or self-determination. We know that you cannot separate politics and faith. Our first aim is to break down stereotypes. The second is to facilitate the meeting of our various congregations. We also try to pray together. In our monthly meetings we ask a cleric — a Jew, a Muslim, a Christian or a Druze — to reflect on peace from a spiritual point of view. We also express solidarity with those suffering injustice in the West Bank and Gaza Strip. We support those seeking medical relief in Israel when the know-how or equipment is unavailable in the Occupied Territories. We work as a group for the right of everyone to religious freedom and to acceptance as part of the Israeli community.

In Israel we have the problem of the politicians debating the question, Who is a Jew? You should know that Conservative and Liberal Jews are not recognized as legitimate branches of Judaism in Israel. They are fighting for their rights, and we support them. We also protest acts like the desecration of a holy place, the burning of churches, synagogues, or mosques by extremists. We pay solidarity visits to such sites too. We all have to recognize that Palestinians and Israelis are destined to live in the same area, and therefore the only way is the way of peace. The Israeli government has tried war many times — in 1948, 1956, 1967, 1973, and 1982 — and has exhausted this option.

Dr. Mahmud al-Zahar

The Islamic movement, which has experienced a resurgence throughout the Islamic world, has also taken its stand against the Occupation. Particularly scornful of Jewish sovereignty in the Middle East, it has vowed to liberate all Palestine, granting Jews and Christians full rights as People of the Book in an Islamic state. Although there has been tension with the secular Palestinian nationalist movement, the various Islamic movements are vigorous in opposing Occupation.

We spoke with Dr. Mahmud al-Zahar, a physician in Gaza City.

Editors: How has the intifada clarified Palestinian thinking about a just solution to the conflict?

Mahmud: The intifada has not provided a solution but rather constitutes a message from the Palestinian people in the Occupied Territories to the Israeli leadership after twenty years of Occupation. All the propaganda concerning the benign Occupation is unacceptable, and the people have risen up to reject the Occupation. This propaganda about economic improvement is simply lies. The difference between a human and an animal is that the human needs dignity, and there is no dignity under Occupation. The message is that we want a solution, and it is a "hot" message. In fact, the message has been sent since the Occupation arrived, as we have been refusing this Occupation continuously and demanding a solution. The intifada came as a "hot" message to the Israelis that there is no way but for a solution and that the Palestinians will not coexist with the Occupation.

You have asked about justice. We take our understanding of justice from the Qur'an and from the Prophet, peace be upon him. Justice says that this land is Islamic. We have lived on this land for thousands of years, and Israel does not have the historical right it claims to have. If we applied historical right in an absolute sense, we would evoke chaos. We would then, as Muslims, return to Spain, a land we left just over four hundred years ago. We would return all the Australians to Europe because they arrived there only one hundred years ago. We would have to leave America to the Red Indians. Historical right is inapplicable and cannot be used by one people against another. If historical right is valid here, then we left Palestine only forty years ago, whereas the Jews left two thousand years ago — so who do you think has the right to return to the land? We need a standard if we are to relate to justice, and that standard must be the teaching of God Almighty. If one seeks to apply justice, one should seek refuge in religion, whether it be Judaism, Christianity, or Islam, for therein there are no differences regarding the perfection of justice. Jews, Christians, and Muslims, if they search for the standard of justice, will see that it is the same in all their religions. This is because the three religions are all from the same source.

What is the material price for which a man is prepared to sacrifice his life? For what is a mother prepared to sacrifice her sons as martyrs? For what price is a mother prepared to see her son killed and then rejoice as if it were his wedding day? Let me tell you that there is no material price, only faith. In Islam the martyr is called by God Almighty. Martyrs are those who are killed while in the path of God. They will be in paradise, in the highest levels, together with their Lord.

Eds.: But there are mothers in the refugee camps who say that they have given their sons for the homeland.

Mahmud: The ignorance of people concerning the nature of Islam leads them to mistaken conclusions. People love their homeland, a specific land and the people living there, but Islam teaches us that every Islamic land is the homeland of every Muslim, and Muslims are commanded to love them all. The meaning of nationalism is much wider in Islam than simple regionalism. There is a difference between those who see all Islamic land as their homeland and all the Islamic people as their people and those who see themselves as only living in Palestine, Lebanon, Egypt, or Syria. Regionalism is one level that exists in Islam, but there is a much wider level. The Islamic tradition is clear about this, as it is written, "The Arab is not preferred to the Persian — preferred is one who fears God." Islam recognizes that there is a pluralism of peoples, but within Islam there is coexistence. The level that is wider than all others and is all-inclusive is the level of religion, or Islam. So now, what is preferable? That I love only Palestine and work for the interests of its people, or that all Islamic land is my homeland and I work for the interests of all its peoples? There is no contradiction between this and loving this land and its people.

Eds.: If a secular Palestinian state is established within the limited borders of the Occupied Territories, what would be the reaction of the Islamic movement?

Mahmud: If the entire people choose a secular regime, then all Muslims would accept that decision. Our one and only condition is that the choice be free and democratic. But Muslims would continue to work for the establishment of an Islamic state peacefully, educating the people concerning the will of God Almighty and the virtues of religion. As it is written, "Call the people to the way of God in wisdom; live as a good example." If the people want to be ruled by a secular regime, we will accept that. As Muslims, please God, we will not enter into conflict with them. But we will continue to call on all the people until they change that secular regime.

Secular regimes like those of America, the Soviet Union, and the Arab countries have brought nothing of benefit to the secularists and have led only to economic, social, and political crisis. Egypt instituted a secular regime — a country with the best land, the best water in the world, the most industrious people — yet it has not been able to accomplish anything from the economic, social, or political point of view. Gorbachev admitted that the Communist regime has failed because it is unsuitable for the people. He tried to change the system by adopting a Western model, but I think that the people on the other side of Europe are not happier than those in the East. Possibly there is a lot of money, but there are a lot of psychological problems.

How can you achieve a stable state? In my opinion, it is only through religion. The religion that contains the fullest details with no distortion is Islam, and therefore we ask you also to try Islam. The trend all over the world is clearly in this direction. In Afghanistan, for example, all the revolutionaries struggling against the regime are Islamic. In Egypt the people are turning toward Islam. Tunisia, Algeria, and recently the election results achieved in Jordan illustrate the same movement. The entire world is turning toward Islam.

Eds.: Yet some say that the Islamic regime has also failed. Look at the government in Iran.

Mahmud: There is a big difference between the so-called Islamic government in Iran and a Sunni Islamic government. The Shi'a system is different from that of the Sunna. The Shi'a system is based upon principles that do not exist in the Sunni system. If you study Islamic history from the time of the prophet until the beginning of this century, you will see that throughout the existence of the Islamic state, other religions were not persecuted, and people were never exiled from their land. If you want to know what the character of the Islamic state will be, then read the Holy Qur'an, the sayings of the Prophet, peace be upon him, but do not derive your impression from any existing regime, for they are based upon flesh and blood. Human beings make mistakes, but the Qur'an is infallible. Please God, we will draw closer to Islam and learn the Qur'an and the sayings even more so that the state we establish will follow the example of that established by Umar bin Khattab, Uthman, Ali, the Umayyads, the Abbasids, and the Ottoman state at the beginning.

Eds.: What do you say to Palestinian Christians who fear this talk of the establishment of an Islamic state?

Mahmud: I am very glad that you have asked this question. Only those Christians who do not know their own Christianity will fear Islam. I want to explain to you the Islamic system concerning the Christians, and the same goes for the Jews. The Jews and the Christians are both *dhimmi* in Islam, which means that they are under the protection of the Muslims. The Prophet, peace be upon him, said, "He who commits aggression against a *dhimmi*, commits aggression against me." This is the teaching to which we are committed. Let us also take an example from Islamic history and the relations between Muslims and Christians. Umar bin 'As, the ruler over Egypt after the Islamic conquest, appointed a Christian as minister of finance. This is what history teaches us; it is not just something we say. We also have the example of the Jarajima, a Christian tribe of soldiers and officers living under the Ottoman Empire who had both the privileges and the duties of Muslims. In addition, when the Crusaders, supposedly Christians, occupied the land, the Christians of Jerusalem joined with their Muslim brothers to fight these Crusaders. This is because they knew the justice of Islam.

Qur'anic teaching respects other religions. Christians who do not know Islam and do not know the history of Christians under Islamic rule should read about Islam. The Muslim treats the People of the Book equitably, whether they are Jews or Christians. Of course one needs to distinguish here between the Jews and the Zionists and remember the Christians who came to attack the Holy Land under the name "Crusaders." Rights are not granted to imperialist Jews or Christians who come to attack the land. Christians who practice their religion under the Islamic regime will be respected a lot more than secular Muslims. The secularists have left their religious community. Often it is these secular regimes that abuse Christians; although the regime may do this in the name of Islam, the regime is not Islamic. One example of this is in the era of Nasser [president of Egypt], who mistreated the Jews of Egypt. But then Nasser cannot be seen as upholding an Islamic regime. The same goes for Tunisia or Algeria or elsewhere. These are not Islamic systems; they are secular, semi-Islamic, or distorted Islamic systems.

Eds.: The role of women has been very clear in the intifada even in the confrontations with the army. What is your opinion of this?

Mahmud: The woman has many roles — student, wife, mother, sister, organizer. In her role as sister and student she has participated for the whole world to see. Her outstanding role is that of mother, one who teaches her son that Islam removes fear, that nothing happens that is not according to the intent of God. It is the mother who participates, through her role as mother, in the sending of this message opposing the Occupation through her son to the Israeli authorities. This role is visible at every stage. When the son is in prison, the roles of the mother and the wife are outstanding indeed.

The role of the woman in Islamic education has been greatly advanced by the Islamic University here in Gaza. When the university adopted Islamic dress for the women students, this was followed by the entire Gaza Strip adopting the Islamic dress code. The women followed this up by refusing to consider marriage to those who did not live according to Islamic law, those who drank alcohol, and so forth, which led to a demand for Islamic bridegrooms. Since the mother understood the role of Islam, the meaning of sacrifice, she no longer took leave of her martyred son with tears but rather ululated and sang like at a wedding. When she understood this, she did not implant fear in the second son, who one day might well follow the first son in this way. Islam has removed fear from the heart of the child, from the heart of the young women, from the heart of the mother, from the heart of the wife, and this allows us to go on, despite the conditions in which we live.

Eds.: After there is an Islamic state, how do you see the relationship between men and women?

Mahmud: In fact there are a number of books that deal with the relations between women and men in Islam. Karima Hamza, a woman, has written *The Trip from Unveiling to the Veil,* in which she talks about her adoption of the hijab, or the Islamic uniform. In fact, if we study Islam properly, we will see that no other regime fulfils women's rights as fully as does the Islamic regime. In the Qur'an, God Almighty says, "Upon them is all that is known." That is to say, they have the same obligations as men. The woman in the Islamic period realized her full rights. Islam regulates completely relations between men and women, and this is not randomly done but through marriage. The Holy Qur'an tells us about her rights in every sphere, as mother, as wife, when she is loved, when she is divorced. If there are difficulties in establishing a stable family life, the man is allowed to take a second wife, but not just at random.

In Islam, a woman may become a doctor, a manufacturer, an educator, even a soldier. My own wife, by the way, is a teacher. I see no contradiction between the woman as a teacher and the woman as a wife. But we cannot destroy children and their psychology because of materialist motivations. The woman must balance her role as wife and mother, responsible for turning out children in the right way, and her other roles.

Do you know that a woman who has a lot of offspring has a reduced chance of getting cancer of the breast, uterus, and cervix? When the woman stopped fulfilling her role of giving birth to children and bringing them up, the diseases attacked. In the Islamic system, we see that the woman is able to preserve her social, economic, and political dignity completely, unlike in any other regime, whether it be Communist, socialist, or capitalist.

Eds.: Have you always been a believer?

Mahmud: Thank God I was never a Communist. But a person passes through many stages, especially as regards the attitude to faith. When I was small, I prayed, but then there were periods when I did not. We lived in the period of Nasser, who taught us that religion was a crime. He taught us that the Muslims were collaborators with America, guilty of injustice and enmity. He taught us that whoever practices religion might be put in prison. There were periods when I did not have the correct understanding. But thank God I have never smoked a cigarette, never drunk a drop of alcohol. Now I am married and have seven children. Now I am Islamic, not just Muslim. The difference between Muslim and Islamic is that if you give the chance to Muslims, they might establish a secular state. But the Islamic person will establish only an Islamic state.

Rabbi Ehud Bandel

A growing number of religious Jews have been challenged by the moral dimensions of the Occupation and the Israeli response to the intifada. Although Jewish religious fundamentalism has tended to side with the Greater Israel movement, quoting biblical legitimation for Jewish sovereignty in the Occupied Territories, a significant religious Jewish peace camp has emerged. Former Sephardi Chief Rabbi Ovadia Yosef has taken a clear stand that human life is more important than land.

We spoke with Conservative Rabbi Ehud Bandel, among the members of Clergy for Peace, an interfaith group composed of Jewish, Muslim, and Christian clergy working for peace, and Rabbinic Human Rights Watch.

Editors: How do you understand the concept of justice in the Israeli-Palestinian conflict in the light of the developments of the past two years?

Ehud: I would like to begin by speaking about a certain turning point that took place in my life. This occurred as a direct result of my own military service in the Occupied Territories. I spent seventy days, divided into two separate periods of reserve duty, in Khan Yunis, in the Gaza Strip. The military service in Khan Yunis was most definitely a turning point in my political thinking, in becoming sensitive to the reality in which we live. I realized that we must reach some political solution that will enable the two peoples who live in this land to live alongside one another. For twenty years of Occupation we were not conscious, we did not take notice of our rule over another people, we did not know that other people. It is this mutual process of awakening to reality that seems to me to be the essence of the intifada.

The first time I arrived in Khan Yunis for my reserve duty during the intifada, I passed into Gaza through Ashqelon, through the Erez checkpoint, and then I felt as if I were in another world. We live here in Israel, and it is so close. At a distance of a few kilometers, suddenly the entire atmosphere changes. You find yourself in a completely different world. I have served many times in the territories during my reserve duty, but always on the main roads. I never had to descend into the alleyways of the refugee camps. The reality of the intifada, however, forced us to enter the narrow alleyways, where we could see the true physical conditions of the people, and I simply could not believe it. I could not believe that conditions like these existed in a modern, developed country. I saw ten people in a room, unpaved roads, sewage flowing in the streets. The most shocking were the nights. We would go out on a night patrol, lighting up the way with a torch. Each time you lighted up some heap, a carpet of rats scattered. You come from a modern, developed world with shopping centers and urban amenities, and only half an hour's journey away you find a completely different world where there is no sanitation.

Then there is the meeting with the residents. For me personally, this led to a sharpening of my political senses. It is simply an impossible situation. I want to emphasize that the situation is impossible because I see myself as a sensitive person, conscious of moral issues and with deeply rooted Jewish concepts — the human being is created in the image and likeness of God, all human beings are equal, and so on. I see myself as alien to racist, Fascist, or chauvinist views. I am active in various frameworks of interfaith understanding, and my own religious approach is one of openness. Yet in this situation I felt myself becoming more and more aggressive and violent. I found myself developing defense systems in order to deal with this reality. Even the most morally sensitive persons, the greatest humanists, are not immune; they have to start swimming with the tide. It is a kind of survival. You stand there in uniform, with a gun in your hand, and already at that point you are no longer discerning what you believe in. You are an enemy. You stand there, and stones are thrown at you and perhaps a Molotov cocktail and sometimes a grenade. What are you supposed to do?

I will give you an example of a moral dilemma faced by our soldiers every day. Part of the Palestinian struggle is to place roadblocks — stones, boards, an old refrigerator — to prevent the army from entering into the alleys. Then a burning tire is placed in the middle. A major part of the soldier's work is to remove these roadblocks. Sometimes there is a fear that these roadblocks are booby-trapped. In that case the soldiers catch the first Arab that they see, usually some old man. The youth manage to get away very fast, and only the old men are left behind. There are clear orders that the soldiers must try to find a young man, but usually the earth seems to have swallowed them up. So the soldiers turn to the old man and order him to remove the roadblock. They are asking him to remove a roadblock that they fear is booby-trapped. In most cases it is not booby-trapped, but the Palestinians will sometimes put a box with wires coming out of it in the middle of the roadblock, just to increase the pressure. But a week ago an Arab who had been ordered to remove a roadblock was seriously wounded. Soldiers often find three of these roadblocks within half an hour, and they have to be removed. Would you go yourself and remove it and endanger your life? Yet why must that poor Arab whom you have caught endanger himself to remove it?

People have stopped getting excited about all this, and this is a natural defense mechanism. When I sensed that this was what was happening to me, even though I have devoted my whole life to studying religion, emphasizing the moral dimension, I began to wonder, What happens to people who are not so steeped in all this study? Suddenly you can understand what happened forty-five years ago in a different country. There is a kind of dynamic that develops and you slowly lose your sensitivity. You stop relating to your enemy as a human being. I am not saying this in a critical way; it is a natural process. In a war you simply cannot relate to the enemy as human beings. Yet you have to stop and ask yourself: "Hey, wait a minute, what is going on here? Where are we headed?" You experience thousands of such incidents during your military reserve duty. You burst into a house to look for somebody who you know is involved in sabotage activity, but can you blame the babies for it? You burst into a house at midnight, and the children wake up and start to cry. And suddenly you see yourself through their eyes. It is as if they are holding up a mirror so that you can see yourself, and your face is suddenly monstrously reflected. What is happening to us?

One incident really broke me. One day we had a case of some graffiti on the walls. You must understand that this writing on the walls is a type of contact sheet that announces that tomorrow or next week there will be a strike to commemorate this or that event. Our orders, aside from catching people when they were writing these notices, were to erase the graffiti and to report the content so that we would be ready if there was a strike or any other activity. We discovered a piece of graffiti that was still freshly painted, as though it had been written just ten minutes before. I caught someone and asked him to read to me what was written. He stood there very frightened. He seemed an intelligent person, well educated, but he claimed he could not read. "You are lying," I said. "Really, I cannot read," he answered. I shouted at him that he was lying. I knew for sure that he was lying and that he definitely knew how to read. I said: "Okay, I will read some of it for you." Since I knew some Arabic, I started to read, "There will be a general strike . . . ," but I did not remember how to read the numbers in Arabic. I said to him, "Read me just the numbers!" He answered that he could not read.

Then this dynamic began to work on me: he knows how to read, and he is lying to me, and I have to get this information out of him. They had given us batons, but I never used one, never even took one with me. I believed that it was beneath me to walk around with a stick in my hand. There was a baton in the jeep. I went and fetched it and came back to the man and said, "If you do not read to me right now what is written, I will. . . . " He simply went down on his knees in front of me and remained absolutely silent. I lifted the baton, and he remained silent. The other soldiers were standing around me, saying, "Come on, beat him!" I froze with the baton in mid-air and caught myself. I looked at them and said: "Leave me alone. You get the information out of him; I'm going." I went, but they eventually succeeded in getting the information out of him. I simply could not be there anymore.

Eds.: Ehud, how do we reach a just solution to this conflict?

Ehud: I have been trying to point out that this passage from the main street to the alleyways, from the statistics to direct contact, has forced the issue. I looked into the Palestinian's eyes, and he was something living, not something abstract. He was living, breathing, suffering, and sighing. I had a few conversations with the children there, and I asked where they are from. I heard, "I am from Jaffa," "I am from Haifa," "I am from . . . ," and they mention names of villages that I have forgotten. From their Arabic names I could decipher their Hebrew names, as these places are known today. These are people who are living with the consciousness that they have been uprooted from their homes, and they cultivate their identity with those same places and same houses in which we Jews live today.

I think here we are all guilty. For the past forty years the Palestinians have been a card in the hands of the Arab states, which have never made the slightest effort to rehabilitate them. Since 1967 they have been living under our rule. All our demagoguery concerning the fact that they never had it so good was exposed by the bitter reality. There is simply glaring injustice, and it is clear that these people are victims of a reality for which we are responsible.

The song "Jerusalem of Gold," by Naomi Shemer, became a national symbol, and it set hearts on fire. It was written in May 1967, before the June war broke out and Jerusalem was united. In one of the verses she says, "The water-holes have dried up, the market-place is empty. Nobody visits the Temple Mount in the Old City." After the 1967 war, she added an additional verse: "We returned to the water-holes, we returned to the market and to the square. A horn sounds on the Temple Mount in the Old City." That is, for nineteen years (from 1948 to 1967) the Old City was supposedly desolate and then suddenly we returned, bringing with us life. Of course the Old City was desolate only in the myth; in reality it was a vibrant Arab center. This explosion of myths is occurring to the whole state.

Years ago Golda Meir stated that there was no such people as the Palestinians, but Menachem Begin, at Camp David, signed accords that speak of the legitimate rights of the Palestinian people. In the Hebrew translation he might call them the Arabs of the Land of Israel, but today everyone knows that there is a Palestinian people. The Israeli right wing concludes that these Palestinians might indeed need a state, but then let them have Jordan. What is important is that twenty years ago, no one even spoke about the Palestinian people. I, too, have reached the conclusion that the Palestinians deserve justice. They are a people that has suffered an injustice. Even if there was no Palestinian nation back in 1948, we created it. From the moment it was created, it had a right to self-determination. It deserves its own state. The intifada was accompanied by the PNC resolutions that overshadowed the Palestinian charter. It was this charter that had called for the destruction of the State of Israel. Today their slogan is "two states for two peoples." They have begun a political process, and we have not had the courage to follow up, but I am sure that we will eventually. I have no doubt that a Palestinian state will be established. I became an activist because I realized that this was inevitable.

Eds.: Was this new awareness an overnight thing?

Ehud: I was aware before. We are all aware. But it did not hit me with this personal impact until the intifada. After seventy days in Khan Yunis, I knew the place better than Jerusalem. You actually live there, you see the people, you meet them. Suddenly, what is going on strikes you. I am sure that other soldiers had similar feelings, but the sad thing is that no one really changes their attitudes. From my experience, and I think it is a known fact, those coming after us are more extreme in their ideology. The process is inevitable, however; two states will exist here side by side, and I only hope that they live in peace together. If this is indeed inevitable, then every day that passes without peace is a terrible injustice. Every drop of blood spilled, whether on our side or theirs, is an unforgivable crime. If we can avoid this bloodshed, then I am obligated by that.

A cornerstone of Judaism is justice: "Justice, justice you shall seek." There is a discussion in the Talmud about compromise. Some say that compromise is sin. Their approach is that compromise distorts the letter of the law. Another approach — in the final analysis, the dominant one — holds that compromise is a value in itself. A ruling in the Talmud, in the Baba Metzia Tractate, applies here. When two people find a prayer shawl and both claim that it is solely theirs, they should share it equitably. The Land of Israel is a prayer shawl that we claimed was all ours, and the Arabs claimed was all theirs. Now we have reached the conclusion that there is no other way: it must be partitioned. The Arabs have taken a historic step forward. Now political wisdom, justice, and morality oblige partition.

I had this awareness in the past, but it was much more theoretical then. This experience of the reality of the intifada and the political steps that accompanied the intifada on the Palestinian side brought me to a degree of activism. Even in the last elections, in 1988, I still voted for the Labour party. I was always among their doves. But today, in the light of Rabin's policies in the Occupied Territories, I have to make a change.

Eds.: Could you explain what you are doing to realize your ideas?

Ehud: Together with some colleagues, other rabbis, we established an organization called the Rabbinic Human Rights Watch. We aimed to focus on the issue of the violation of human rights, principally in the territories, focusing on questions like health. Even the right wing cannot justify injustice in this field. Infant mortality is so high, and the state of the hospitals is shocking. I had a terrible shock upon entering Nasr Hospital in Khan Yunis; you could faint just from the smell. In a modern civilized state how can there be such gaps between our hospitals, in which we take such pride? We send medical assistance to every place in the world, to Romania, to Armenia, we send planes thousands of kilometers to offer medical assistance, we treat children wounded in Armenia or in Chernobyl, when at the same time, a few kilometers from our homes, people are dying because they lack reasonable medical treatment. This is something that religion cannot put up with.

As rabbis, we also confront the violation of rights in the religious sphere. For example, I wrote a letter concerning an incident where soldiers were situated next to a mosque and they used the pages of a Qur'an as toilet paper. We must remember that when it comes to demoralizing the enemy, the consequences will not stop at the Green Line. Our society will be affected too. This rejection of the other soon spreads to all those who do not think like you, who disagree with your political opinions, whose skin color is different, whose religion is different. It does not stop.

I try to convince others by using this moral-pragmatic argument. Some cannot be convinced by pure ethical morality. Pragmatically, what is this Occupation doing to us? We are talking about a dangerous change in character. Recently a report was published by a pathologist working in the Abu Kabir Institute for Forensic Medicine, in which he said that after examining corpses — both Jews and Arabs — he found signs of greater violence within Israeli society than in the previous two years. He believed that there was a connection between this violence and political conflict. There is a numbing of the senses; you simply stop being sensitive. This pathologist expressed surprise at seeing soldiers bring in a mother to identify the decomposed remains of her son. They just stood there indifferently as if they had lost all sensitivity. I do not blame them. You have to survive, and it is like in the Holocaust; you see the pictures of the ghetto with bodies lying in the streets. People go to and fro and do not even look at the corpses; it is a daily thing, and people do not get excited anymore. But what kind of psychological distortion does this cause a person who has become blocked to pain?

I see here processes developing that remind me too much of Europe in the 1940s, with all the obvious differences. I just heard a lecture about how to teach the Holocaust, and the central message was that we must not demonize the Nazis. The minute you demonize the Nazis, it distances you from them; it seems as though you are talking about creatures from another planet. But Nazi Germany is this planet, and nobody is immune to this. As soon as you demonize, you immunize yourself and say, in effect, it cannot happen to me. These are monsters, not human beings. The solutions proposed by Hitler (may his name be erased) seemed so logical, so reasonable, so real, and therefore he rose to power democratically. What happens to a whole people convinced by this machinery?

Eds.: How do you relate this to your religious life?

Ehud: Judaism has an image of mending the world. We conclude our prayers three times a day with, "It is upon us to praise. . . ." This particular prayer contains an internal contradiction. Within the second part we ask "to mend the world under the Kingdom of the Almighty," and the wording is very universal, but the first part stresses that we thank God "because he has not made us like the Gentiles." This is very particularistic, even chauvinistic. We are not like them, "bowing to idols"; this shows the superiority of the Jews, the Chosen People. But our vision does not end with this particularism. It is rather a vision of our mission in connection with the whole world.

I think the particularism tries to teach us that there are no short cuts. You cannot go out to mend the world before you mend yourself; you have to build your own society based on justice, and then you need not use missionaries, because that society will radiate its own light. This is what it means when we say, "Light to the nations." It does not mean we come and say, "Hey, nations, I came to give you light." No, it means that if you build your society on justice, it will radiate. You must start with yourself, your family, your neighborhood, your town, your state, and the world will follow.

Glossary

Terminology concerning the land and the people is very sensitive in the Israeli-Palestinian conflict. Jews and Palestinians may refer to the same place using different names (Shechem/Nablus, Ashdod/Isdud, Yaffo/Jaffa, Hebron/al-Khalil, etc.). Naming is part of the conflict itself. Whereas some Israeli Jews refer to the areas occupied by the Israeli army in 1967 as Judea, Samaria, and Gaza, some Palestinians refer to these areas as Occupied Palestine (the State of Palestine was declared in November 1988). These are the areas referred to generally as the Occupied Territories, which include the West Bank and Gaza Strip. Some Israeli Jews refer to the residents of these territories as Arabs, undifferentiated from other Arabs in Saudi Arabia, Egypt, or Syria, whereas the residents identify themselves as Palestinians. Throughout the introduction and the interviews we have followed the terminology of the person interviewed, trying to be sensitive to issues of national identity and gender.

Aliyah: Hebrew word meaning "ascent," which refers to Jewish immigration to Israel. Immigrants are referred to as "olim."

Ashkenazi: "Ashkenaz" refers to Germany, but the term includes all Jews who originate in the lands of Northern and Eastern Europe. The largest communities in Israel are those from Poland, Romania, and the Soviet Union.

Awdah: Arabic word meaning "return"; see Right of Return.

Balfour Declaration: A declaration issued in 1917 by the British government just before the British invasion of Palestine, promising "the establishment in Palestine of a National Home for the Jews."

Begin, Menachem: Prime minister of Israel from 1977 until 1983, leader of the right-wing Herut party and head of the Likud bloc. Begin retired from political life after the Lebanon War.

Ben-Gurion, David: Veteran Zionist leader and first prime minister of Israel after the establishment of the state in 1948.

Collaborators: Palestinians from the Occupied Territories who assist the Israeli military authorities in maintaining the Occupation. Dozens of collaborators have been killed by Palestinians during the intifada.

Deir Yassin: A Palestinian village near Jerusalem where Jewish underground militias massacred over 250 people in April 1948 just before the establishment of the State of Israel. The event terrified many Palestinians, who subsequently fled their homes.

Democratic Front for the Liberation of Palestine (DFLP): A leftist group in the PLO headed by Naif Hawatmeh.

Diaspora: A Greek word implying dispersion. For Jews, this refers to the dispersion of the Jews throughout the world following the destruction of the Second Temple in Jerusalem in 70 C.E. To Palestinians, this refers to the dispersion of the Palestinian people after the 1948 war.

Druze: A religious community based primarily in Lebanon, Syria, and Israel. The Druze broke with Shi'a Islam in the eleventh century. Their doctrines combine Islamic, Neoplatonic, and Judeo-Christian themes and are shrouded in secrecy.

Dunam: A unit of land measure equal to one thousand square meters (about one-quarter acre).

Fatah: The centrist party in the PLO, headed by Yasser Arafat.

Feda'in: Arabic word meaning "those who sacrifice themselves for their country," referring to Palestinian guerrillas who committed acts of sabotage against Israel, particularly after the establishment of the PLO.

Gaza Strip: Territory on the Mediterranean coast occupied by the Israelis in 1967. Formerly administered by Egypt, this territory with over 650,000 people is extremely densely populated with Palestinian refugees from the 1948 war.

Golan Heights: A mountainous region on Syria's border with Israel, occupied by the Israelis in 1967. The present inhabitants are members of the Druze religion who consider themselves Syrians and resist Israeli occupation.

Green Line: This refers to the 1948–49 borders, which demarcate the boundary between the State of Israel and the Occupied Territories.

Gush Emunim: Hebrew phrase meaning "the bloc of the faithful," the name of a popular movement that supports Jewish settlement in, and Jewish annexation of, the Occupied Territories.

HAMAS: An Arabic acronym for the Islamic resistance movement. An organization of resurgent Muslims who demand both an end to the Occupation and the creation of an Islamic state in Palestine. Certain elements demand an end to the State of Israel. The organization is banned by the Israelis, who consider HAMAS membership a security offense.

Holocaust: The catastrophe that engulfed European Jewry during the Second World War. Initiated by the Nazis inspired by Adolf Hitler, six million Jews throughout Europe were murdered, and millions more were incarcerated in concentration camps and ghettos. The survivors became refugees dispersed throughout the world, many finding a haven in Israel.

Hussein, King: King of Jordan since 1953 and ruler of the West Bank until 1967, when it was occupied by Israel.

Intifada: An Arabic word used to describe the uprising of Palestinians in the Occupied Territories against Israeli military rule there. The word implies the attempt to shake off something troublesome or irritating. Palestinians mark the beginning of the uprising as December 9, 1987.

Kafr Qasim: A Palestinian village in central Israel where the Israeli army shot dead forty-nine people returning from work in the fields at the outbreak of the 1956 war.

Knesset: Israel's 120-member parliament.

Labour party: More correctly, the Labour Alignment, a coalition of socialist center and left-of-center political parties. Some form of Labour ideology has ruled Israel since 1948. Although Labour lost power in 1977, it returned to share power with the Likud in 1984. The present head of the Labour Alignment is Shimon Peres.

Law of Return: A law promulgated by the Israeli parliament in 1950 enabling any Jew to claim immediate citizenship in Israel upon taking up residency there.

Likud: An Israeli coalition of rightist political parties headed at present by Yitzhaq Shamir. Led to electoral victory by Menachem Begin in 1977, the Likud has been sharing power in Israel with the Labour party since 1984.

Moshav: Hebrew word meaning "settlement," referring to a variety of agricultural villages and cooperatives established in Israel.

National Unified Leadership: The leadership of the intifada, which includes all branches of the Palestinian national movement. This body is underground, its membership unknown. It directs the opposition to the Occupation through clandestinely distributed leaflets proclaiming general strikes, days of confrontation, and other activities.

Oriental Jews: Refers to those Jews who originate from the Orient, including the Jews of the Arab countries. These Jews comprise the majority in Israel today, the two largest communities being the Moroccan and Iraqi Jews. Often used interchangeably with the term "Sephardis."

Palestine Liberation Organization (PLO): An umbrella Palestinian organization founded in 1964 that includes various groups of Palestinian nationalists. The organization is at present headed by Yasser Arafat, named president of Palestine in 1989. The organization is banned in Israel and in the Occupied Territories, and membership in or support for the organization is considered a security offense punishable by imprisonment.

Palestine National Congress (PNC): The supreme forum of the Palestinian resistance organizations, consisting of representatives from the Palestinian Diaspora and from the Occupied Territories. The congress meets once every few years. This is considered the parliament of the Palestinian people and is presently headed by Sheikh Abd al-Hamid al-Sayegh.

Peres, Shimon: Leader of the Labour party and Alignment bloc and head of the Israeli opposition. Peres has held numerous positions in Israeli governments.

Phalangists: A right-wing, predominantly Maronite Christian militia in Lebanon, noted for its anti-Palestinian positions.

Popular Front for the Liberation of Palestine (PFLP): A leftist group in the PLO headed by George Habash.

Qur'an (Koran): For Muslims this is Holy Scripture, revealed by God to the Prophet Muhammad through the agency of the Archangel Gabriel over a number of years.

Right of Return: The Palestinians who live as refugees outside of their homeland demand the right to return either to a state of their own in Palestine or to the homes they left as a result of the war between Israel and the Arab armies.

Sabra and Shatila: Two Palestinian refugee camps in Beirut where Lebanese Phalangist forces massacred hundreds of people in retribution for the assassination of Bashir Gemayel. Many saw Israel as responsible for having allowed the Phalangists freedom of movement following the Israeli occupation of Beirut.

Sephardis: "Sepharad" refers to the lands of the Iberian Peninsula — Spain and Portugal. The term includes all Jews who originate from these lands but who were expelled during the fifteenth century and migrated to many lands including North Africa, Turkey, and Palestine. It is often used interchangeably with the term "Oriental Jews."

Settlers: Israeli Jews who have built their homes in the Occupied Territories since 1967. These settlers are motivated by a mixture of religious nationalism, a preference for Jewish rule in these territories, and economic incentives provided by the government in the form of cheap housing.

Shabab: Arabic word meaning "youth." Within the context of the intifada, it refers to Palestinian youth who are involved in anti-Occupation activities.

Shamir, Yitzhaq: Present Israeli prime minister and political successor of Menachem Begin, previously noted for his extreme right-wing views.

Torah: For Jews this refers either to all of Holy Scripture, the Hebrew Bible and the Talmud, or solely to the first five books of the Hebrew Bible, known as the Pentateuch.

Two-States Solution: Proposal to solve the Israeli-Palestinian conflict through the establishment of a Palestinian state in the Occupied Territories alongside the State of Israel.

United Nations Resolutions: The United Nations has been involved in the Israeli-Palestinian conflict from the beginning. In 1947 the United Nations voted in favor of partition. In 1948 its Resolution 194 called for negotiations and a solution to the problem of the refugees. In 1967 Resolution 242 called for the "establishment of a just and lasting peace," a withdrawal of Israeli armed forces from territories occupied, the termination of belligerency, and recognition of all states in the area and their right to live in peace with secure borders.

Wars: There have been numerous wars between Israel and its Arab neighbors — in 1948, 1956, 1967, 1973, and 1982. There have also been periods of intense military confrontation that are not referred to as wars. Many of the wars are referred to differently by Jews and Arabs. The 1948 war is known by Jews as the War of Independence and by Palestinians as the Disaster. The 1967 war is known as the Six-Day War by Jews. The 1982 Lebanon War is officially called the Campaign for the Peace of Galilee in Israel.

West Bank: Territory on the west bank of the Jordan River, occupied by Israel in 1967. At its center is Arab Jerusalem (annexed by the Israelis) and Bethlehem, with Nablus in the north and Hebron in the south. Containing over nine hundred thousand Palestinian residents, the area is referred to by some as Judea and Samaria, biblical names of the area. The territory was formerly ruled by Jordan.

Yesh Gvul: Hebrew phrase meaning "there is a limit"; it is the name of an organization of Israeli soldiers opposing military service in the Occupied Territories and demanding alternative military service within the Green Line.

Zionism: A Jewish national movement founded in nineteenth-century Europe, inspired by European nationalism and the Jewish religion. Minimally, Zionism proposes that the sole hope for continued Jewish survival is the existence of a Jewish state in Israel and the possibility for all Jews to immigrate there.

Recommended Reading

Ateek, Naim. *Justice and Only Justice: A Palestinian Theology of Liberation*. Maryknoll, N.Y.: Orbis Books, 1989.

Birkland, Carol. *Unified in Hope: Arabs and Jews Talk about Peace*. New York: Friendship Press, 1987.

Chacour, Elias. *Blood Brothers*. Old Tappan, N.J.: Revell, 1984.

Ellis, Marc. *Toward a Jewish Theology of Liberation*. Maryknoll, N.Y.: Orbis Books, 1989.

Flappan, Simha. *The Birth of Israel: Myths and Realities*. New York: Pantheon Books, 1987.

Grossman, David. *The Yellow Wind*. London: J. Cape, 1988.

Khalidi, Walid. *Before Their Diaspora*. Washington, D.C.: Institute for Palestine Studies, 1984.

Oz, Amos. *In the Land of Israel*. Toronto: Collins Publishers, 1988.

Ruether, Rosemary Radford, and Herman Ruether. *The Wrath of Jonah*. San Francisco: Harper & Row, 1989.

Said, Edward. *The Question of Palestine*. New York: Random House, Vintage Books, 1980.

Sayigh, Rosemary. *Palestinians: From Peasants to Revolutionaries*. London: Zed Press, 1979.

Schiff, Ze'ev, and Ehud Ya'ari. *Intifada*. New York: Simon and Schuster, 1990.